GAS PHASE ION CHEMISTRY

GAS PHASE ION CHEMISTRY

By
Amit Arora

DISCOVERY PUBLISHING HOUSE PVT. LTD.
NEW DELHI-110 002

Published by:
Tilak Wasan

DISCOVERY PUBLISHING HOUSE PVT. LTD.
4831/24, Ansari Road, Prahlad Street
Darya Ganj, New Delhi-110002 (India)
Phone: +91-11-23279245, 43764432
Fax: +91-11-23253475
E-mail: parul.wasan@gmail.com
discoverypublishinghouse@gmail.com
info@discoverypublishinggroup.com
web: www.discoverypublishinggroup.com

First Edition: **2011**
ISBN: 978-81-8356-770-1

Gas Phase ION Chemistry

Printed at:
Shree Balaji Art Press
Delhi

Preface

Gas phase ion chemistry is a field of science encompassed within both chemistry and physics. It is the science that studies ions and molecules in the gas phase, most often enabled by some form of mass spectrometry. By far the most important applications for this science is in studying the thermodynamics and kinetics of reactions. For example one application is in studying the thermodynamics of the solvation of ions. Ions with small solvation spheres of 1, 2, 3 . . . solvent molecules can be studied in the gas phase and then extrapolated to bulk solution.

All gases have observable properties in common:

- Gases flow readily from one space to another and occupy all available space.
- Gases assume the shapes of their containers.
- Gases are readily compressible. By exerting force, we can cause a gas to occupy a smaller volume.
- Two or more gases form homogeneous mixtures (solutions) in all proportions. An example is air, a mixture of primarily nitrogen and oxygen with small amounts of other gases.

- Gases diffuse rapidly. This means that a gas can move across a large space in a relatively short time. Examples are the odors of perfume and skunk.

The state of a gas is described by the values of 4 macroscopic variables: the volume (V) occupied by the gas; the temperature (T) of the gas; the pressure (P) that the gas exerts on the walls of its container; and the amount of gas in moles (n). The values of these quantities are related by a very simple equation called the ideal gas law.

Author

Contents

1 Introduction

Gas phase ion chemistry is a field of science encompassed within both chemistry and physics. It is the science that studies ions and molecules in the gas phase, most often enabled by some form of mass spectrometry. By far the most important applications for this science is in studying the thermodynamics and kinetics of reactions. For example one application is in studying the thermodynamics of the solvation of ions. Ions with small solvation spheres of 1, 2, 3 . . . solvent molecules can be studied in the gas phase and then extrapolated to bulk solution.

Theory

RRKM Theory

RRKM theory is used to compute simple estimates of the unimolecular reaction rates from a few characteristics of the potential energy surface.

Gas Phase Ion Formation

The process of converting an atom or molecule into an ion by adding or removing charged particles such as electrons or other ions can occur in the gas phase. These processes are an important component of gas phase ion chemistry.

Associative Ionization

Associative ionization is a gas phase reaction in which two atoms or molecules interact to form a single product ion.

$$A^{*} + B \rightarrow AB^{+\bullet} + e^{-}$$

where species A with excess internal energy (indicated by the asterisk) interacts with B to form the ion AB^{+}.

One or both of the interacting species may have excess internal energy.

Charge-exchange Ionization

Charge-exchange ionization (also called charge-transfer ionization) is a gas phase reaction between an ion and a neutral species.

$$A^{+} + B \rightarrow A + B^{+}$$

in which the charge of the ion is transferred to the neutral.

Chemical Ionization

In chemical ionization, ions are produced through the reaction of ions of a reagent gas with other species. Some common reagent gases include: methane, ammonia, and isobutane.

Chemi-ionization

Chemi-ionization can be represented by

$$G^{*} + M \rightarrow M^{+\bullet} + e^{+} + G$$

where G is the excited state species (indicated by the superscripted asterisk), and M is the species that is ionized by the loss of an electron to form the radical cation (indicated by the superscripted "plus-dot").

Penning Ionization

Penning ionization refers to the interaction between a gas-phase excited-state atom or molecule G* and a target molecule M resulting in the formation of a radical molecular cation M+., an electron e-, and a neutral gas molecule G

$$G^{*} + M \rightarrow M^{+\bullet} + e^{+} + G$$

Penning ionization occurs when the target molecule has an ionization potential lower than the internal energy of the excited-state atom or molecule. Associative Penning ionization can also occur:

$$G^{*} + M \rightarrow MG^{+\bullet} + e^{-}$$

Fragmentation

There are many important dissociation reactions that take place in the gas phase.

Collision-induced Dissociation

CID (also called collisionally activated dissociation - CAD) is a method used to fragment molecular ions in the gas phase. The molecular ions collide with neutral gas molecules such as helium, nitrogen or argon. In the collision some of the kinetic energy is converted into internal energy which results in fragmentation.

Charge Remote Fragmentation

Charge remote fragmentation is a type of covalent bond breaking that occurs in a gas phase ion in which the cleaved bond is not adjacent to the location of the charge.

Transition State Theory

Transition state theory (TST) is a theory that explains the reaction rates of elementary chemical reactions. The theory assumes a special type of chemical equilibrium (quasi-equilibrium) between reactants and activated transition state complexes.

TST is primarily used as a qualitative basis to understand how chemical reactions take place. TST has been less successful in its original goal of calculating absolute reaction rate constants because of the fact that the calculation of absolute reaction rates requires very accurate knowledge of potential energy surfaces but it has been successful in calculating the standard enthalpy of activation , the standard entropy of activation and the standard Gibbs energy of activation for a particular reaction if its rate constant has been experimentally determined. (The ‡ notation refers to the value of interest *at the transition state*.)

This theory was developed simultaneously in 1935 by Henry Eyring, then at Princeton University, and by Meredith Gwynne TST is also referred to as "activated-complex theory"

Before the development of TST, the Arrhenius rate law was widely used to determine energies for the reaction barrier. The Arrhenius equation arises from empirical observation and ignores any mechanistic considerations, such as whether one or more reactive intermediates are involved in the overall conversion of a reactant to a product Therefore, further development was necessary to understand the two parameters associated with this law, the pre-exponential factor (A) and the activation energy (Ea). TST which led to the Eyring equation successfully addresses these two issues; however, 46 years elapsed between the publication of the Arrhenius rate law in 1889 and Eyring equation based on TST in 1935. Over this period of time work of many scientists and researchers contributed significantly to the development of this theory.

Theory

Basic ideas behind the transition state theory are as follows:

1. Rates of the reactions are studied by studying activated complexes which lie at the col (saddle point) of a

potential energy surface. The details of how the complexes are formed are not important.

2. The activated complexes are in a special equilibrium (quasi-equilibrium) with the reactant molecules.
3. The activated complexes can convert into products which allows kinetic theory to calculate the rate of this conversion.

Development

In the development of TST, three approaches were taken as summarized below:

Thermodynamic Treatment

In 1884, Jacobus van't Hoff proposed the Van't Hoff equation describing the temperature dependence of the equilibrium constant for a reversible reaction:

$$A \leftrightarrows B$$

$$\frac{d\ln K}{dT} = \frac{\Delta U}{RT^2}$$

where ΔU is the change in internal energy, K is the equilibrium constant of the reaction, R is the universal gas constant, and T is thermodynamic temperature. Based on experimental work, in 1889, Svante Arrhenius proposed a similar expression for the rate constant of a reaction, given as follows:

$$\frac{d\ln K}{dT} = \frac{\Delta E}{RT^2}$$

Integration of this expression leads to the Arrhenius equation

$$k = Ae^{\frac{-E}{RT}}$$

A was referred to as the frequency factor (now called the pre-exponential coefficient), and *E* is regarded as the activation energy. By the early 20th century many had accepted the Arrhenius equation, but the physical interpretation of *A* and *E* remained vague. This led many researchers in chemical kinetics to offer different theories of how chemical reactions occurred in an attempt to relate *A* and *E* to the molecular dynamics directly responsible for chemical reactions.

In 1910, Rene Marcelin introduced the concept of standard Gibbs energy of activation. His equation can be written as

$$k \alpha \exp\left(\frac{\Delta^{\ddagger} G^{\ominus}}{RT}\right)$$

At about the same time as Marcelin was working on his formulation, Dutch chemists Philip Abraham Kohnstamm, Frans Eppo Cornelis Scheffer, and Wiedold Frans Brandsma introduced for the first time standard entropy of activation and the standard enthalpy of activation. They proposed the following rate constant equation

$$k \alpha \exp\left(\frac{\Delta^{\ddagger} S^{\ominus}}{R}\right) \exp\left(\frac{-\Delta^{\ddagger} H^{\ominus}}{RT}\right)$$

However, the nature of the constant was still unclear.

Kinetic-Theory Treatment

In early 1900, Max Trautz and William Lewis studied the rate of the reaction using collision theory, based on the kinetic theory of gases. Collision theory treats reacting molecules as hard spheres colliding with one another; this theory neglects entropy changes.

Lewis applied his treatment to the following reaction and obtained good agreement with experimental result.

$2HI \rightarrow H_2 + I_2$

However, later when the same treatment was applied to other reactions, there were large discrepancies between theoretical and experimental results.

Statistical-Mechanical Treatment

Statistical mechanics played a significant role in the development of TST. However, the application of statistical mechanics to TST was developed very slowly given the fact that in mid 1800s, James Clerk Maxwell, Ludwig Boltzmann, and Leopold Pfaundler published several papers discussing reaction equilibrium and rates in terms of molecular motions and the statistical distribution of molecular speeds.

It was not until 1912 when the French chemist A. Berthoud used Maxwell-Boltzmann distribution law to obtain an expression for the rate constant.

$$\frac{d \ln k}{dT} = \frac{a - bT}{RT^2}$$

where a and b are constants related to energy terms.

Two years later, Marcelin made an essential contribution by treating the progress of a chemical reaction as a motion of a point in phase space. He then applied Gibbs' statistical-mechanical procedures and obtained an expression similar to the one which he had obtained earlier from thermodynamic consideration.

In 1915, another important contribution came from British physicist James Rice. Based on his statistical analysis, he concluded that the rate constant is proportional to the "critical increment". His ideas were further developed by Tolman. In 1919, Austrian physicist Karl Ferdinand Herzfeld applied statistical mechanics to the equilibrium constant and kinetic theory to the rate constant of the reverse reaction, k_{-1}, for the reversible dissociation of a diatomic molecule.

$$AB \underset{k_{-1}}{\overset{k_1}{\rightleftarrows}} A + B$$

He obtained the following equation for the rate constant of the forward reaction

$$k_1 = \frac{k_B T}{h}\left(1 - \exp\left(\frac{-hv}{k_B T}\right)\right)\exp\left(\frac{-E^{\Theta}}{RT}\right)$$

where E^{Θ} is the dissociation energy at absolute zero, k_B is the Boltzmann constant, h is the Planck constant, T is thermodynamic temperature, ? is vibrational frequency of the bond. This expression is very important since it is the first time that the factor $k_B T/h$, which is a critical çomponent of TST, has appeared in a rate equation.

In 1920, the American chemist Richard Chase Tolman further developed Rice's idea of the critical increment. He concluded that critical increment (now referred to as activation energy) of a reaction is equal to the average energy of all molecules undergoing reaction minus the average energy of all reactant molecules.

Potential Energy Surfaces

The concept of potential energy surface was very important in the development of TST. The foundation of this concept was laid by Marcelin. He theorized that the progress of a chemical reaction could be described as a point in a potential energy surface with coordinates in atomic momenta and distances.

In 1931, Eyring and Polanyi constructed a potential energy surface for the reaction below. This surface is a three-dimensional diagram based on quantum-mechanical principles as well as experimental data on vibrational frequencies and energies of dissociation.

$$H + H_2 \rightarrow H_2 + H$$

A year after the Eyring and Polanyi construction, H. Pelzer and Eugene Wigner made an important contribution by following the progress of a reaction on a potential energy surface. The importance of this work was that it was the first time that the concept of col or saddle point in the potential energy surface was discussed. They concluded that the rate of a reaction is determined by the motion of the system through that col.

Limitations of Transition State Theory

In general, TST has provided researchers with a conceptual foundation for understanding how chemical reactions take place. Even though the theory is widely accepted, it does have limitations. For example, the theory assumes that once the transition structure proceeds down the potential energy surface, it leads to one product (or one set of products). However, in some reactions, the transition state may traverse the potential energy surface in such a way, that it leads to an unexpected product selectivity not predicted by transition state theory (an example of such a reaction is the thermal decomposition of diazaobicyclopentanes, presented by Anslyn and Doughtery).

Transition state theory is also based on the assumption that atomic nuclei behave according to classic mechanics. It is assumed that unless atoms or molecules collide with enough energy to form the transition structure, then the reaction does not occur. However, according to quantum mechanics, for any barrier with a finite amount of energy, there is a possibility that particles can still tunnel across the barrier. With respect to chemical reactions this means that there is a chance that molecules will react even if they do not collide with enough energy to traverse the energy barrier. While this effect is expected to be negligible for reactions with large activation energies, it becomes a more important phenomenon for reactions with relatively low energy barriers, since the tunneling probability increases with decreasing barrier height.

Transition state theory fails for some reactions at high temperature. The theory assumes the reaction system will pass over the lowest energy saddle on the potential energy surface. Recall that the highest point of this saddle is called the transition state. While this description is consistent for reactions occurring at relatively low temperatures, at high temperatures, molecules populate higher energy vibrational modes; their motion becomes more complex and collisions may lead to transition states far away from that predicted by transition state energy. This deviation from transition state theory is observed even in the simple exchange reaction between diatomic hydrogen and a hydrogen radical.

Given these limitations, several alternatives to transition state theory have been proposed. A brief discussion of these theories follows.

Generalized Transition State Theory (TST)

Any form of TST, such as microcanonical variational TST, canonical variational TST, and improved canonical variational TST, in which the transition state is not necessarily located at the saddle point, is referred to as generalized transition state theory.

Microcanonical Variational TST

A development of transition state theory in which the dividing surface is varied so as to minimize the rate calculated for a fixed energy. The rate expressions obtained in a microcanonical treatment can be integrated over the energy, taking into account the statistical distribution over energy states, so as to give the canonical, or thermal rates.

Canonical Variational TST

A development of transition state theory in which the position of the dividing surface is varied so as to minimize the rate constant at a given temperature.

Improved Canonical Variational TST

A modification of canonical variational transition state theory in which, for energies below the threshold energy, the position of the dividing surface is taken to be that of the microcanonical threshold energy. This forces the contributions to rate constants to be zero if they are below the threshold energy. A compromise dividing surface is then chosen so as to minimize the contributions to the rate constant made by reactants having higher energies.

ION

An ion is an atom or molecule where the total number of electrons is not equal to the total number of protons, giving it a net positive or negative electrical charge.

Since protons are positively charged and electrons are negatively charged, if there are more electrons than protons, the atom or molecule will be negatively charged. This is called an **anion** from the Greek word *'ano'*, meaning 'up'.

Conversely, if there are more protons than electrons, the atom or molecule will be positively charged. This is called a cation from the Greek word *'kata'*, meaning 'down'.

An ion consisting of a single atom is called a *monatomic ion*. If it consists of two or more atoms, it is called a *polyatomic ion*. Polyatomic ions containing oxygen, such as carbonate and sulfate, are called oxyanions.

When writing the chemical formula for an ion, its charge is written as a superscript '+' or '–' following a number indicating the difference between the number of protons and the number of electrons. The number is omitted if it is equal to 1. For example, the sodium cation is written as Na^+, the

'+' indicating that it has one less electron than it has protons. The sulfate anion is written as SO_4^{2-}, the '2−' indicating that it has *two* more electrons than it has protons. If an ion contains unpaired electrons, it is called a radical ion. Just like neutral radicals, radical ions are very reactive.

Formation

Formation of Monatomic Ions

Monatomic ions are formed by the addition of electrons to the valence shell of the atom, or the losing of electrons from this shell. The inner shells of an atom are filled with electrons that are tightly bound to the positively-charged atomic nucleus, and so do not participate in this kind of chemical interaction. The process of gaining or losing electrons from a neutral atom or molecule is called ionization.

Atoms can be ionized by bombardment with radiation, but the more usual process of ionization encountered in chemistry is the transfer of electrons between atoms or molecules. This transfer is usually driven by the attaining of stable ("closed shell") electronic configurations. For example, a sodium atom, Na, has a single electron in its valence shell, surrounding a stable, closed inner shell of 10 electrons. Since the 10-electron configuration is very stable, sodium "likes" to lose its extra electron so that it can attain to this stable configuration, becoming the sodium cation in the process:

$$Na \rightarrow Na^+ + e^O$$

On the other hand, a chlorine atom, Cl, has 7 electrons in its valence shell, which is one short of the stable, filled shell with 8 electrons. Thus, chlorine "likes" to *gain* an extra electron in order to attain to the stable 8-electron configuration, becoming the chloride anion in the process:

$$Cl + e^O \rightarrow Cl^-$$

This driving force is what causes sodium and chlorine to undergo a chemical reaction, where the "extra" electron is transferred from sodium to chlorine, forming sodium cations and chloride anions. Being oppositely-charged, these cations and anions combine together to form sodium chloride, NaCl, more commonly known as salt.

$$Na^{+} + Cl^{-} \rightarrow Nacl$$

Formation of Polyatomic and Molecular Ions

Polyatomic and molecular ions are often formed by the gaining or losing of elemental ions such as H^+ in neutral molecules. For example, when ammonia, NH_3, accepts a proton, H^+, it forms the ammonium ion, NH_4^+. Ammonia and ammonium have the same number of electrons in essentially the same electronic configuration, but ammonium has an extra proton that gives it a net positive charge.

Ammonia can also lose an electron to gain a positive charge, forming the ion $\bullet NH_3$. However, this ion is unstable, because it has an incomplete valence shell around the nitrogen atom, making it a very reactive radical ion.

Due to the instability of radical ions, polyatomic and molecular ions are usually formed by gaining or losing elemental ions such as H^+, rather than gaining or losing electrons. This allows the molecule to preserve its stable electronic configuration while acquiring an electrical charge.

Ionization Potential

The energy required to detach an electron in its lowest energy state from an atom or molecule of a gas with less net electric charge is called the *ionization potential*, or *ionization energy*. The *n*th ionization energy of an atom is the energy required to detach its *n*th electron after the first *n - 1* electrons have already been detached.

Each successive ionization energy is markedly greater than the last. Particularly great increases occur after any given block of atomic orbitals is exhausted of electrons. For this reason, ions tend to form in ways that leave them with full orbital blocks. For example, sodium has one *valence electron*, in its outermost shell, so in ionized form it is commonly found with one lost electron, as Na^+. On the other side of the periodic table, chlorine has seven valence electrons, so in ionized form it is commonly found with one gained electron, as Cl^-. Caesium has the lowest measured ionization energy of all the elements and helium has the greatest. The ionization energy of metals is generally much lower than the ionization energy of nonmetals, which is why metals will generally lose electrons to form positively-charged ions while nonmetals will generally gain electrons to form negatively-charged ions.

Ionic Bonding

Ionic bonding is a kind of chemical bonding that arises from the mutual attraction of oppositely-charged ions. Since ions of like charge repel each other, they do not usually exist on their own. Instead, they are bound to ions of the opposite charge. The resulting compound is called an *ionic compound*, and is said to be held together by *ionic bonding*.

The most common type of ionic bonding is seen in compounds of metals and nonmetals (except noble gases, which rarely form chemical compounds). Metals are characterized by having a small number of electrons in excess of a stable, closed-shell electronic configuration. As such, they have the tendency to lose these extra electrons in order to attain to the stable configuration. This property is known as *electropositivity*. Non-metals, on the other hand, are characterized by having an electron configuration just a few electrons short of a stable configuration. As such, they have the tendency to gain more electrons in order to attain to the stable configuration. This tendency is known as *electronegativity*. When a highly electropositive metal is combined with a highly electronegative nonmetal, the extra electrons from the metal atoms are transferred to the electron-deficient nonmetal atoms. This reaction produces metal cations and nonmetal anions, which are attracted to each other to form a *salt*.

Common Cations			Common Anions		
Common Name	Formula	Historic Name	Formula Name	Formula	Alt. Name
Simple Cations			*Simple Anions*		
Aluminium	Al^{3+}	alumen	Chloride	Cl^-	
Calcium	Ca^{2+}	calx	Fluoride	F^-	
Copper(ll)	Cu^{2+}	cupric	Hydride H^- Oxide	O^{2-}	
Iron(ll)	Fe^{2+}	ferrous	Sulfide Oxoanions	$S2^-$	
Iron(lll)	Fe^{3+}	ferric	Carbonate	CO_3^{2-}	
Magnesium	Mg^{2+}	magnesia	Hydrogen carbonate	HCO_3^-	Bicarbonate
Mercury(ll)	Hg^{2+}	mercuric	Hydroxide	OH^-	
Potassium	K^+	potash	Nitrate	NO^{3-}	
Silver	Ag^+	siolfur	Nitrite	NO^{3-}	
Sodium	Na^+	soda	Phosphate	PO_4^{3-}	
Polyatomic Cations			**Sulfate Thiosulfate**	$SO_4S_2O_3$	
Ammonium	NH_4^+		*Anions from Organic Acids*		
Hydronium	H_3O^+		Acetate	$C_3H_3O_3^-$	
Mercury(l)	Hg_3^{2+}	mercurous	Formate	HCO_3^-	
			Oxalate	$C_3O_4^{2-}$	
			Cyanide	CN^-	

Plasma

A collection of non-aqueous gas-like ions, or even a gas containing a proportion of charged particles, is called a plasma, often called the *fourth state of matter* because its properties are quite different from solids, liquids, and gases. Astrophysical plasmas containing predominantly a mixture of electrons and protons, may make up as much as 99.9% of visible matter in the universe.

Applications

Ions are essential to life. Sodium, potassium, calcium and other ions play an important role in the cells of living organisms, particularly in cell membranes. They have many practical, everyday applications in items such as smoke detectors, and are also finding use in unconventional technologies such as ion engines. Inorganic dissolved ions are a component of total dissolved solids, an indicator of water quality in the world.

In physics, a gas is a state of matter, consisting of a collection of particles (molecules, atoms, ions, electrons, etc.) without a definite shape or volume that are in more or less random motion.

Physical Characteristics

Due to the electronic nature of the aforementioned particles, a "force field" is present throughout the space around them. Interactions between these "force fields" from one particle to the next give rise to the term intermolecular forces. Dependent on distance, these intermolecular forces influence the motion of these particles and hence their thermodynamic properties. At the temperatures and pressures characteristic of many applications, these particles are normally greatly separated. This separation corresponds to a very weak attractive force. As a result, for many applications, this intermolecular force becomes negligible.

A gas also exhibits the following characteristics:

- Relatively low density and viscosity compared to the solid and liquid states of matter.
- Will expand and contract greatly with changes in temperature or pressure, thus the term "compressible".
- Will diffuse readily, spreading apart in order to homogeneously distribute itself throughout any container.

Macroscopic

When analyzing a system, it is typical to specify a length scale. A *larger* length scale may correspond to a macroscopic view of the system, while a *smaller* length scale corresponds to a microscopic view.

On a macroscopic scale, the quantities measured are in terms of the *large scale* effects that a gas has on a system or its surroundings such as its velocity, pressure, or temperature. Mathematical equations, such as the Extended hydrodynamic equations, Navier-Stokes equations and the Euler equations have been developed to attempt to model the relations of the pressure, density, temperature, and velocity of a moving gas.

Pressure

The pressure exerted by a gas uniformly across the surface of a container can be described by simple kinetic theory. The particles of a gas are constantly moving in random directions and frequently collide with the walls of the container and/or each other. These particles all exhibit the physical properties of mass, momentum, and energy, which all must be conserved. In classical mechanics, *Momentum*, by definition, is the product of mass and velocity. Kinetic energy is one half the mass multiplied by the square of the velocity.

The sum of all the normal components of force exerted by the particles impacting the walls of the container divided by the area of the wall is defined to be the pressure. The pressure can then be said to be the average linear momentum of these moving particles. A common misconception is that the collisions of the molecules with each other is essential to explain gas pressure, but in fact their random velocities are sufficient to define this quantity.

Temperature

The temperature of any physical system is the result of the motions of the molecules and atoms which make up the system. In statistical mechanics, temperature is the measure of the average kinetic energy stored in a particle. The methods of storing this energy are dictated by the degrees of freedom of the particle itself (energy modes). These particles have a range of different velocities, and the velocity of any single particle constantly changes due to collisions with other particles. The range in speed is usually described by the Maxwell-Boltzmann distribution.

Specific Volume

When performing a thermodynamic analysis, it is typical to speak of intensive and extensive properties. Properties which depend on the amount of gas are called *extensive* properties, while properties that do not depend on the amount of gas are called *intensive* properties. Specific volume is an example of an *intensive* property because it is the volume occupied by a *unit of mass* of a material, meaning the volume has been divided through by the mass in order to obtain a quantity in terms of, for example

$$\frac{m^3}{kg}$$

Notice that the difference between volume and specific volume differ in that the specific quantity is mass *independent*.

Density

Because the molecules are free to move about in a gas, the mass of the gas is normally characterized by its density. Density is the mass per volume of a substance or simply, the inverse of specific volume. For gases, the density can vary over a wide range because the molecules are free to move. Macroscopically, density is a state variable of a gas and the change in density during any process is governed by the laws of thermodynamics. Given that there are many particles in completely random motion, for a static gas, the density is the same throughout the entire container. Density is therefore a scalar quantity; it is a simple physical quantity that has a magnitude but no direction associated with it. It can be shown by kinetic theory that the density is proportional to the size of the container in which a fixed mass of gas is confined.

Volume

The volume of gas increases proportionally to absolute temperature and decreases inversely proportionally to pressure, approximately according to the ideal gas law. It may be expressed as total volume of a gas mixture, or as partial gas volume of any individual gas component.

Microscopic

On the microscopic scale, the quantities measured are at the molecular level. Different theories and mathematical models have been created to describe molecular or particle motion. A few of the gas-related models are listed below.

Kinetic Theory

Kinetic theory attempts to explain macroscopic properties of gases by considering their molecular composition and motion.

Brownian Motion

Brownian motion is the mathematical model used to describe the random movement of particles suspended in a fluid often called particle theory.

Since it is at the limit of (or beyond) current technology to observe individual gas particles (atoms or molecules), only theoretical calculations give suggestions as to how they move, but their motion is different from Brownian Motion. The reason is that Brownian Motion involves a smooth drag due to the frictional force of many gas molecules, punctuated by violent collisions of an individual (or several) gas molecule(s) with the particle. The particle (generally consisting of millions or billions of atoms) thus moves in a jagged course, yet not so jagged as would be expected if an individual gas molecule was examined.

Intermolecular Forces

As discussed earlier, momentary attractions (or repulsions) between particles have an effect on gas dynamics. In physical chemistry, the name given to these intermolecular forces is *van der Waals force*.

Simplified Models

An *equation of state* (for gases) is a mathematical model used to roughly describe or predict the state of a gas. At present, there is no single equation of state that accurately predicts the properties of all gases under all conditions. Therefore, a number of much more accurate equations of state have been developed for gases under a given set of assumptions. The "gas models" that are most widely discussed are "Real Gas", "Ideal Gas" and "Perfect Gas". Each of these models have their own set of assumptions to facilitate the analysis of a given thermodynamic system.

Real Gas

Real gas effects refers to an assumption base where the following are taken into account:

- Compressibility effects
- Variable heat capacity
- Van der Waals forces
- Non-equilibrium thermodynamic effects
- Issues with molecular dissociation and elementary reactions with variable composition.

For most applications, such a detailed analysis is excessive. An example where "Real Gas effects" would have a significant impact would be on the Space Shuttle re-entry where extremely high temperatures and pressures are present.

Ideal Gas

An "ideal gas" is a simplified "real gas" with the assumption that the compressibility factor Z is set to 1. So the state variables follow the ideal gas law.

This approximation is more suitable for applications in engineering although simpler models can be used to produce a "ball-park" range as to where the real solution should lie. An example where the "ideal gas approximation" would be suitable would be inside a combustion chamber of a jet engine. It may also be useful to keep the elementary reactions and chemical dissociations for calculating emissions.

Perfect Gas

By definition, A perfect gas is one in which intermolecular forces are neglected. So, along with the assumptions of an *Ideal Gas*, the following assumptions are added:

- Neglected intermolecular forces

By neglecting these forces, the equation of state for a *perfect gas* can be simply derived from kinetic theory or statistical mechanics.

This type of assumption is useful for making calculations very simple and easy to do. With this assumption, the *Ideal gas law* can be applied without restriction and many complications that may arise from the Van der Waals forces can be neglected.

Along with the definition of a perfect gas, there are also two more simplifications that can be made although various textbooks either omit or combine the following simplifications into a general "perfect gas" definition. For sake of clarity, these simplifications are defined separately.

Thermally Perfect

Thermally Perfect Gas

- The gas is in Thermodynamic equilibrium
- Not chemically reacting
- Internal energy, Enthalpy, and Specific Heat are functions of Temperature *only*.

$e = e(T)$ $h = h(T)$ $de = C_v dT$ $dh = C_p dT$

This type of approximation is useful for modeling, for example, an axial compressor where temperature fluctuations are usually not large enough to cause any significant deviations from the *Thermally perfect* gas model. Heat capacity is still allowed to vary, though only with temperature and molecules are not permitted to dissociate.

Calorically Perfect

The Calorically perfect gas model is the most restrictive as it applies all the previous assumptions expressed in the *Thermally perfect* model and also adds:

- Constant Specific Heats

$e = C_v T$ $h = C_p T$

Although this may be the most restrictive model, it still may be accurate enough to make reasonable calculations. For example, if a model of one compression stage of the axial compressor mentioned in the previous example was made (one with variable C_p, and one with constant C_p) to compare the two simplifications, the deviation may be found at a small enough order of magnitude that other factors that come into play in this compression would have a greater impact on the final result than whether or not C_p was held constant. (compressor tip-clearance, boundary layer/frictional losses, manufacturing impurities, etc.)

Historical Synthesis

Boyle's Law

Boyle's Law was perhaps the first expression of an equation of state. In 1662 Robert Boyle, an Irishman, performed a series of experiments employing a J-shaped glass tube, which was sealed on one end. Mercury was added to the tube, trapping a fixed quantity of air in the short, sealed end of the tube. Then the volume of gas was carefully measured as additional mercury was added to the tube. The pressure of the gas could be determined by the difference between the mercury level in the short end of the tube and that in the long, open end. Through these experiments, Boyle noted that the gas volume varied inversely with the pressure. In mathematical form, this can be stated as: $pV = constant$.

This law is used widely to describe different thermodynamic processes by adjusting the equation to read $pVn = constant$ and then varying the n through different values such as the specific heat ratio?

Charles' Law

In 1787 the French physicist Jacques Charles found that oxygen, nitrogen, hydrogen, carbon dioxide, and air expand to the same extent over the same 80 kelvin interval.

Law of Volume

In 1802, Joseph Louis Gay-Lussac published results of similar experiments, indicating a linear relationship between volume and temperature:

$$V_1/T_1 = V_2/T_2$$

Dalton's Law

In 1801 John Dalton published the Law of Partial Pressures: The pressure of a mixture of gases is equal to the sum of the pressures of all of the constituent gases alone. Mathematically, this can be represented for n species as:

$$Pressure_{total} = Pressure_1 + Pressure_2 + \ldots + Pressure_n$$

Compressibility

The compressibility factor (Z) is used to alter the ideal gas equation to account for the real gas behavior. It is sometimes referred to as a "fudge-factor" to make the ideal gas law more accurate for the application. *Usually* this Z value is very close to unity.

Reynolds Number

In fluid mechanics, the Reynolds number is the ratio of inertial forces ($v_s\rho$) to viscous forces (μ/L). It is one of the most important dimensionless numbers in fluid dynamics and is used, usually along with other dimensionless numbers, to provide a criterion for determining dynamic similitude.

Viscosity

Pressure acts perpendicular (normal) to the wall. The tangential (shear) component of the force that is left over is related to the *viscosity* of the gas. As an object moves through a gas, viscous effects become more prevalent.

Turbulence

In fluid dynamics, turbulence or turbulent flow is a flow regime characterized by chaotic, stochastic property changes. This includes low momentum diffusion, high momentum convection, and rapid variation of pressure and velocity in space and time.

Boundary Layer

Particles will, in effect, "stick" to the surface of an object moving through it. This layer of particles is called the boundary layer. At the surface of the object, it is essentially static due to the friction of the surface. The object, with its boundary layer is effectively the new shape of the object that the rest of the molecules "see" as the object approaches. This boundary layer *can* separate from the surface, essentially creating a new surface and completely changing the flow path. The classical example of this is a stalling airfoil.

Maximum Entropy Principle

As the total number of degrees of freedom approaches infinity, the system will be found in the macrostate that corresponds to the highest multiplicity.

Thermodynamic Equilibrium

Equilibrium thermodynamics applies if the energy change within a system occurs on a timescale large enough for a sufficient number of molecular collisions to occur so that the energy transfer between molecules and between energy modes to allow the new energy value to be distributed in equilibrium among the molecules. (For typical systems, this is on the order of a few nanoseconds)

NATURAL GAS

Natural gas is a gas consisting primarily of methane. It is found associated with fossil fuels, in coal beds, as methane clathrates, and is created by methanogenic organisms in marshes, bogs, and landfills. It is an important fuel source, a major feedstock for fertilizers, and a potent greenhouse gas.

Natural gas is often informally referred to as simply gas, especially when compared to other energy sources such as electricity. Before natural gas can be used as a fuel, it must undergo extensive processing to remove almost all materials other than methane. The by-products of that processing include ethane, propane, butanes, pentanes and higher molecular weight hydrocarbons, elemental sulfur, and sometimes helium and nitrogen.

Sources

Fossil Natural Gas

In the 1800s, natural gas was usually produced as a byproduct of producing oil, since the small, light gas carbon chains come out of solution as it undergoes pressure reduction from the reservoir to the surface, similar to uncapping a bottle of soda pop where the carbon dioxide effervesces. Unwanted natural gas can be a disposal problem at the well site. If there is not a market for natural gas near the wellhead it was virtually valueless since it must be piped to the end user. In the 1800s and early 1900s, such unwanted gas was usually burned off at the well site. Often, wanted gas (or 'standard' gas without a market) is pumped back into the reservoir with an 'injection' well for disposal or repressurizing the producing formation. Another solution is to export the natural gas as a liquid. Gas-to-liquid, (GTL) is a developing technology that converts standard natural gas into synthetic gasoline, diesel or jet fuel through the Fischer-Tropsch process developed in World War II Germany. Such fuels can be transported through conventional pipelines and tankers to users. Proponents claim GTL fuels burn cleaner than comparable petroleum fuels. Most major international oil companies are in advanced development stages of GTL production, with a world-scale (14,000 bbl/day) GTL plant in Qatar scheduled to come online before 2010. In locations such as the United States with a high natural gas demand, pipelines are constructed to take the gas from the wellsite to the end consumer.

Fossil natural gas can be "associated" (found in oil fields) or "non-associated" (isolated in natural gas fields), and is also found in coal beds (as coalbed methane). It sometimes contains significant quantities of ethane, propane, butane, and pentane—heavier hydrocarbons removed prior to use as a consumer fuel—as well as carbon dioxide, nitrogen, helium and hydrogen sulfide Natural gas is commercially produced from oil fields and natural gas fields. Gas produced from oil wells is called casinghead gas or associated gas. The natural gas industry is producing gas from increasingly more challenging resource types: sour gas, tight gas, shale gas and coalbed methane.

The world's largest proven gas reserves are located in Russia, with 4.757×10^{13} m^3 (1.6×10^{15} cu ft). Russia is also the world's largest natural gas producer, through the Gazprom company. Major proven resources (with year of estimate) (in billion cubic metres) are world 175,400 (2006), Russia 47,570 (2006), Iran 26,370 (2006), Qatar 25,790 (2007), Saudi Arabia 6,568 (2006) and United Arab Emirates 5,823 (2006).

The world's largest gas field is Qatar's offshore North Field, estimated to have 25 trillion cubic metres (9.0 □ 10^{14} cu ft) of gas in place—enough to last more than 200 years at optimum production levels. The second largest natural gas field is the South Pars Gas Field in Iranian waters in the Persian Gulf. Connected to Qatar's North Field, it has estimated reserves of 8 to 14 trillion cubic metres (2.8×10^{14} to 5.0×10^{14} cu ft) of gas.

Because natural gas is not a pure product, when non-associated gas is extracted from a field under supercritical (pressure/temperature) conditions, it may partially condense upon isothermic depressurizing—an effect called retrograde condensation. The liquids thus formed may get trapped by depositing in the pores of the gas reservoir. One method to deal with this problem is to reinject dried gas free of condensate to maintain the underground pressure and to allow reevapouration and extraction of condensates.

Town Gas

Town gas is a mixture of methane and other gases, mainly the highly toxic carbon monoxide, that can be used in a similar way to natural gas and can be produced by treating coal chemically. This is a historic technology, still used as 'best solution' in some local circumstances, although coal gasification is not usually economic at current gas prices. However, depending upon infrastructure considerations, it remains a future possibility.

Most town "gashouses" located in the eastern United States in the late nineteenth and early twentieth centuries were simple by-product coke ovens which heated bituminous coal in air-tight chambers. The gas driven off from the coal was collected and distributed through town-wide networks of pipes to residences and other buildings where it was used for cooking and lighting purposes. (Gas heating did not come into widespread use until the last half of the twentieth century.) The coal tar that collected in the bottoms of the gashouse ovens was often used for roofing and other waterproofing purposes, and also, when mixed with sand and gravel, was used for creating Bitumen for the surfacing of local streets.

Biogas

When methane-rich gases are produced by the *anaerobic decay* of non-fossil organic matter (biomass), these are referred to as biogas (or natural biogas). Sources of biogas include swamps, marshes, and landfills (see landfill gas), as well as sewage sludge and manure by way of anaerobic digesters, in addition to enteric fermentation particularly in cattle.

Methanogenic archaea are responsible for all biological sources of methane, some in symbiotic relationships with other life forms, including termites, ruminants, and cultivated crops. Methane released directly into the atmosphere would be considered a pollutant, however, methane in the atmosphere is oxidised, producing carbon dioxide and water. Methane in the atmosphere has a half life of seven years, meaning that every seven years, half of the methane present is converted to carbon dioxide and water.

Future sources of *methane,* the principal component of natural gas, include landfill gas, biogas and methane hydrate. Biogas, and especially landfill gas, are already used in some areas, but their use could be greatly expanded. Landfill gas is a type of biogas, but biogas usually refers to gas produced from organic material that has not been mixed with other waste.

Landfill gas is created from the decomposition of waste in landfills. If the gas is not removed, the pressure may get so high that it works its way to the surface, causing damage to the landfill structure, unpleasant odor, vegetation die-off and an explosion hazard. The gas can be vented to the atmosphere, flared or burned to produce electricity or heat. Experimental systems were being proposed for use in parts Hertfordshire, UK and Lyon in France.

Once *water vapour* is removed, about half of landfill gas is methane. Almost all of the rest is carbon dioxide, but there are also small amounts of nitrogen, oxygen and hydrogen. There are usually trace amounts of hydrogen sulfide and siloxanes, but their concentration varies widely. Landfill gas cannot be distributed through natural gas pipelines unless it is cleaned up to the same quality. It is usually more economical to combust the gas on site or within a short distance of the landfill using a dedicated pipeline. Water vapour is often removed, even if the gas is combusted on site. If low temperatures condense water out of the gas, siloxanes can be lowered as well because they tend to condense out with the water vapour. Other non-methane components may also be removed in order to meet emission standards, to prevent fouling of the equipment or for environmental considerations. Co-firing landfill gas with natural gas improves combustion, which lowers emissions.

Biogas is usually produced using agricultural waste materials, such as otherwise unusable parts of plants and manure. Biogas can also be produced by separating organic materials from waste that otherwise goes to landfills. This is more efficient than just capturing the landfill gas it produces. Using materials that would otherwise generate no income, or even cost money to get rid of, improves the profitability and energy balance of biogas production.

Anaerobic lagoons produce biogas from manure, while biogas reactors can be used for manure or plant parts. Like landfill gas, biogas is mostly methane and carbon dioxide, with small amounts of nitrogen, oxygen and hydrogen. However, with the exception of pesticides, there are usually lower levels of contaminants.

Hydrates

Huge quantities of natural gas (primarily methane) exist in the form of hydrates under sediment on offshore continental shelves and on land in arctic regions that experience permafrost such as those in Siberia (hydrates require a combination of high pressure and low temperature to form). However, as of 2009 no technology has been developed to produce natural gas economically from hydrates.

Natural Gas Processing

The image is a schematic block flow diagram of a typical natural gas processing plant. It shows the various unit processes used to convert raw natural gas into sales gas pipelined to the end user markets.

The block flow diagram (*see on page 32*) also shows how processing of the raw natural gas yields byproduct sulfur, byproduct ethane, and natural gas liquids (NGL) propane, butanes and natural gasoline (denoted as pentanes +).

Uses of Natural Gas

Power Generation

Natural gas is a major source of electricity generation through the use of gas turbines and steam turbines. Most grid peaking power plants and some off-grid engine-generators use natural gas. Particularly high efficiencies can be achieved through combining gas turbines with a steam turbine in combined cycle mode. Natural gas burns more cleanly than other fossil fuels, such as oil and coal, and produces less carbon dioxide per unit energy released. For an equivalent amount of heat, burning natural gas produces about 30% less carbon dioxide than burning petroleum and about 45% less than burning coal Combined cycle power generation using natural gas is thus the cleanest source of power available using fossil fuels, and this technology is

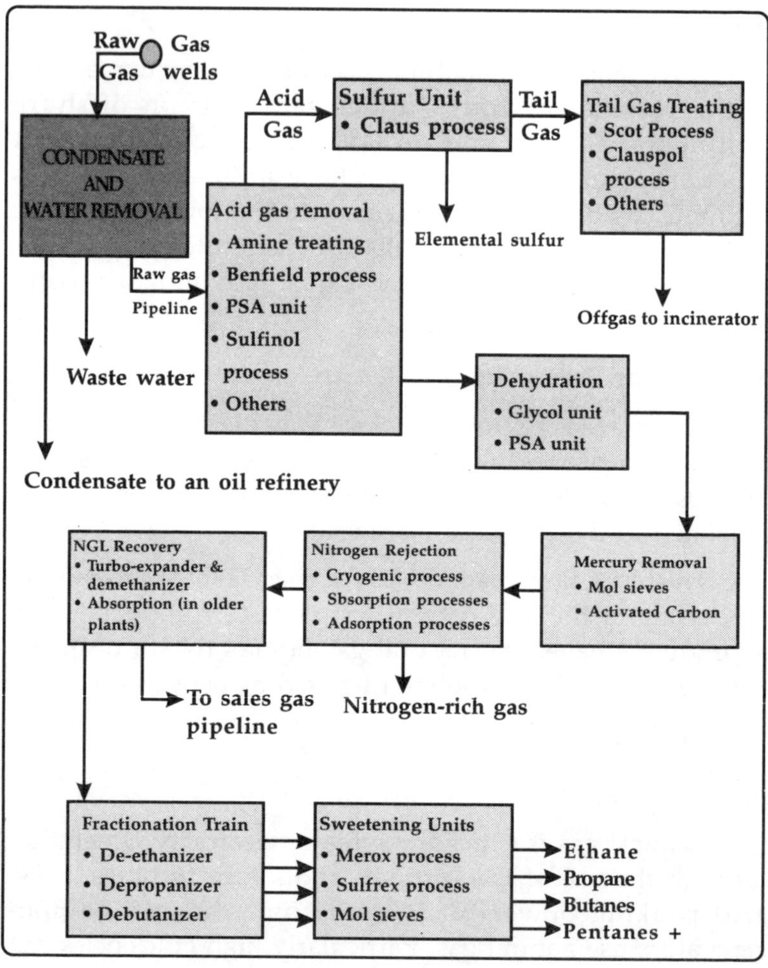

widely used wherever gas can be obtained at a reasonable cost. Fuel cell technology may eventually provide cleaner options for converting natural gas into electricity, but as yet it is not price-competitive.

Domestic Use

Natural gas is supplied to homes, where it is used for such purposes as cooking in natural gas-powered ranges and/or ovens, natural gas-heated clothes dryers, heating/cooling and central heating. Home or other building heating may include boilers, furnaces, and water heaters. CNG is used in rural homes without connections to piped-in public utility services, or with portable grills. However, due to CNG being less economical than LPG, LPG (Propane) is the dominant source of rural gas.

Transportation

Compressed natural gas (CNG) (methane) is a cleaner alternative to other automobile fuels such as gasoline (petrol) and diesel. As of 2005, the countries with the largest number of natural gas vehicles were Argentina, Brazil, India, Pakistan, Italy, Iran, and the United States. The energy efficiency is generally equal to that of gasoline engines, but lower compared with modern diesel engines. Gasoline/petrol vehicles converted to run on natural gas suffer because of the low compression ratio of their engines, resulting in a cropping of delivered power while running on natural gas (10%-15%). CNG-specific engines, however, use a higher compression ratio due to this fuel's higher octane number of 120-130.

Fertilizer

Natural gas is a major feedstock for the production of ammonia, via the Haber process, for use in fertilizer production.

Aviation

Russian aircraft manufacturer Tupolev is currently running a development program to produce LNG- and hydrogen-powered aircraft The program has been running since the mid-1970s, and seeks to develop LNG and hydrogen variants of the Tu-204 and Tu-334 passenger aircraft, and also the Tu-330 cargo aircraft. It claims that at current market prices, an LNG-powered aircraft would cost

5,000 roubles (~ $218/ £112) less to operate per ton, roughly equivalent to 60%, with considerable reductions to carbon monoxide, hydrocarbon and nitrogen oxide emissions.

The advantages of liquid methane as a jet engine fuel are that it has more specific energy than the standard kerosene mixes and that its low temperature can help cool the air which the engine compresses for greater volumetric efficiency, in effect replacing an intercooler. Alternatively, it can be used to lower the temperature of the exhaust.

Hydrogen

Natural gas can be used to produce hydrogen, with one common method being the hydrogen reformer. Hydrogen has various applications: it is a primary feedstock for the chemical industry, a hydrogenating agent, an important commodity for oil refineries, and a fuel source in hydrogen vehicles.

Other

Natural gas is also used in the manufacture of fabrics, glass, steel, plastics, paint, and other products.

Storage and Transport

The major difficulty in the use of natural gas is transportation and storage because of its low density. Natural gas pipelines are economical, but are impractical across oceans. Many existing pipelines in North America are close to reaching their capacity, prompting some politicians representing colder areas to speak publicly of potential shortages.

LNG carriers can be used to transport liquefied natural gas (LNG) across oceans, while tank trucks can carry liquefied or compressed natural gas (CNG) over shorter distances. They may transport natural gas directly to end-users, or to distribution point r cost, requiring additional facilities for liquefaction or compression at the production point, and then gasification or decompression at end-use facilities or into a pipeline.

The gas is now re-injected back into the formation for later recovery. This also assists oil pumping by keeing underground pressures higher. In Saudi Arabia, in the late 1970s, a "Master Gas System" was created, ending the need for flaring. Satellite observation unfortunately shows that some large gas-producing countries still use flaring and venting routinely. The natural gas is used to generate electricity and heat for desalination. Similarly, some landfills that also discharge methane gases have been set up to capture the methane and generate electricity.

Natural gas is often stored underground inside depleted gas reservoirs from previous gas wells, salt domes, or in tanks as liquefied natural gas. The gas is injected during periods of low demand and extracted during periods of higher demand. Storage ner the ultimate end-users helps to best meet volatile demands, but this may not always be practicable.

With 15 nations accounting for 84% of the worldwide production, access to natural gas has become a significant factor in international economics and politics. In this respect, control over the pipelines is a major strategic factor. n particular, in the 200s, Gazprom, the Russian national energy company, has engaged in disputes with Ukraine and Belarus over the price of its natural gas, which have created worries that gas deliveries to parts of Europe could be cut off for political reasons.

Environmental Effects

Global Climate Change

Natural gas is often described as the cleanest fossil fuel, producing less carbon dioxide (CO_2) per joule delivered than either coal or oil However, in absolute terms it does contribute substantially to global emissions, and this contribution is projected to grow. According to the IPCC Fourth Assessment Report in 2004 natural gas produced about 5,300 Mt/yr of CO_2 emissions, while coal and oil produced 10,600 and 10,200 respectively ; but by 2030, according to an updated version of the SRES B2 emissions scenario, natural gas would be the source of 11,000 Mt/yr, with coal and oil now 8,400 and 17,200 respectively.

In addition, natural gas itself is a greenhouse gas far more potent than carbon dioxide when released into the atmosphere but is not of large concern due to the small amounts in which this occurs.

When drilled in the US, the CO_2 pumped out with the natural gas is released directly into the atmosphere. This amount of CO_2 is not counted with the release of the CO_2 when natural gas is burned.

Safety

In any form, a minute amount of odorant such as t-butyl mercaptan, with a rotting-cabbage-like smell, is added to the otherwise colorless and almost odorless gas, so that leaks can be detected before a fire or explosion occurs. Sometimes a related compound, thiophane is used, with a rotten-egg smell. Adding odorant to natural gas began in the United States after the 1937 New London School explosion. The buildup of gas in the school went unnoticed, killing three hundred students and faculty when it ignited. Odorants are considered non-toxic in the extremely low concentrations occurring in natural gas delivered to the end user.

In mines, where methane seeping from rock formations has no odor, sensors are used, and mining apparatuses have been specifically developed to avoid ignition sources, e.g., the Davy lamp.

Explosions caused by natural gas leaks occur a few times each year. Individual homes, small businesses and boats are most frequently affected when an internal leak builds up gas inside the structure. Frequently, the blast will be enough to significantly damage a building but leave it standing. In these cases, the people inside tend to have minor to moderate injuries. Occasionally, the gas can collect in high enough quantities to cause a deadly explosion, disintegrating one or more buildings in the process. The gas usually dissipates readily outdoors, but can sometimes collect in dangerous quantities if weather conditions are right. However, considering the tens of millions of structures that use the fuel, the individual risk of using natural gas is very low.

Some gas fields yield *sour gas* containing hydrogen sulfide (H_2S). This untreated gas is toxic. Amine gas treating, an industrial scale process which removes acidic gaseous compcnents, is often used to remove hydrogen sulfide from natural gas.

Extraction of natural gas (or oil) leads to decrease in pressure in the reservoir. This in turn may lead to subsidence at ground level. Subsidence may affect ecosystems, waterways, sewer and water supply systems, foundations, etc.

While it is assumed that natural gas heating systems are the leading cause of *carbon monoxide* deaths in the United States, it is simply not the case. According to the US Consumer Product Safety Commission (2008), 56% of unintentional deaths from non-fire CO poisoning were associated with engine-driven tools like gas-powered generators and lawn mowers. Natural gas heating systems accounted for 4% of these deaths.

Even though improvements in natural gas furnace designs have greatly reduced CO poisoning concerns, it is still a good idea to have it checked by a heating professional on a regular basis. Detectors are also available that warn of carbon monoxide and/or explosive gas (methane, propane, etc.).

Energy Content, Statistics and Pricing

Quantities of natural gas are measured in normal cubic metres (corresponding to 0 °C at 101.325 kPa) or in standard cubic feet (corresponding to 60 °F (16 °C) and 14.73 PSIA). The gross heat of combustion of one normal cubic meter of commercial quality natural gas is around 39 megajoules (~10.8 kWh), but this can vary by several percent.

The price of natural gas varies greatly depending on location and type of consumer. In 2007, a price of $7 per 1,000 cubic feet (28 m^3) was typical in the United States. The typical caloric value of natural gas is roughly 1,000 BTU per cubic foot, depending on gas composition. This corresponds to around $7 per million BTU, or around $7 per gigajoule. In April 2008, the wholesale price was $10 per 1,000 cubic feet (28 m3) ($10/MMBTU) The residential price varies from 50% to 300% more than the wholesale price. At the end of 2007, this was $12-$16 per 1,000 cu ft (28 m^3) Natural gas in the United States is traded as a futures contract on the New York Mercantile Exchange. Each contract is for 10,000 MMBTU (gigajoules), or 10 billion BTU. Thus, if the price of gas is $10 per million BTUs on the NYMEX, the contract is worth $100,000.

United Kingdom

Natural gas is also traded as a commodity in Europe, principally at the United Kingdom NBP and related European hubs, such as the TTF in the Netherlands.

United States

In US units, one standard cubic foot of natural gas produces around 1,028 British Thermal Units (BTU). The actual heating value when the water formed does not condense is the net heat of combustion and can be as much as 10% less.

In the United States, retail sales are often in units of therms (th); 1 therm = 100,000 BTU. Gas meters measure the volume of gas used, and this is converted to therms by multiplying the volume by the energy content of the gas used during that period, which varies slightly over time. Wholesale transactions are generally done in decatherms (Dth), or in thousand decatherms (MDth), or in million decatherms (MMDth). A million decatherms is roughly a billion cubic feet of natural gas.

Rest of the World

In the rest of the world, LNG (liquified natural gas) and LPG (liquified petroleum gas) is traded in metric tons or mmBTU as spot deliveries. Long term contracts are signed in metric tons. The LNG and LPG is transported by specialized transport ships, as the gas is liquified at cryogenic temperatures. The specification of each LNG/LPG cargo will usually contain the energy content, but this information is in general not available to the public.

3

The Gas Phase

In this chapter we begin an examination of the phases (physical states) in which a pure substance may exist. For most substances there are three phases — solid (s), liquid (l), and gas (g). The gas phase is the simplest of the three to deal with theoretically, primarily because the molecules behave completely chaotically and therefore give rise to simply-formulated average properties. The solid phase is also relatively easily dealt with, because it is so highly organized. The liquid phase, intermediate in its degree of order, is the most difficult to model. This chapter deals with the gas phase. A subsequent chapter deals with the solid and liquid phases. We follow the chapter on the liquid phase with chapters on the energetics of conversions among phases, and equilibria between two or more phases. Of interest throughout will be the question, "Why do some substances exist as solids, some as liquids, and still others as gases at room temperature and subjected to 1 atmosphere of pressure?"

Gases and their properties play an ubiquitous and critical role in our daily lives. Life is supported by the oxygen of the air, which reacts with glucose in biochemical combustion. Living systems have evolved complex molecular architecture to absorb oxygen from the air; carry it to the cells; deliver it to the cells; transport it within the cell; and supervise its multistep, controlled reaction with glucose. It is the rapid expansion of gases produced in the explosive combustion of gasoline that performs the work of the internal combustion engine. Expansion and contraction of gases in response to temperature and pressure changes is at the basis of continually changing weather patterns. Clearly an understanding of the properties, behavior, and chemical reactivity of gases is an important foundation for developing an appreciation of complex biological and technological systems. These properties, behaviors, and reactivities are the focus of this chapter. Following a discussion of the ideal gas law, a simple mathematical model for gas behavior, we discuss the Kinetic Molecular Theory of gases, which establishes a link between molecular motion and temperature. We finish the chapter with a look at the historical significance of gas phase chemical reactions in chemistry, and a treatment of double displacement reactions that produce gases as products.

Macroscopic Properties of Gases

All gases have observable properties in common:

- Gases flow readily from one space to another and occupy all available space.
- Gases assume the shapes of their containers.
- Gases are readily compressible. By exerting force, we can cause a gas to occupy a smaller volume.
- Two or more gases form homogeneous mixtures (solutions) in all proportions. An example is air, a mixture of primarily nitrogen and oxygen with small amounts of other gases.

Gases diffuse rapidly. This means that a gas can move across a large space in a relatively short time. Examples are the odors of perfume and skunk.

The state of a gas is described by the values of 4 macroscopic variables: the volume (V) occupied by the gas; the temperature (T) of the gas; the pressure (P) that the gas exerts on the walls of its container; and the amount of gas in moles (n). The values of these quantities are related by a very simple equation called the ideal gas law. We will discuss this equation after a brief word on pressure.

Pressure

Pressure is defined as force per unit area. We illustrate the concept of pressure with an example.

Gases exert pressure on the walls of their containers. Since a gas uniformly occupies a container, it exerts the same pressure on all the walls. The gases that make up the atmosphere exert pressure on the surface of the earth. This pressure, called the atmospheric pressure, can be measured using a barometer, (*Fig. 3.1*) A glass tube of length 1 m and cross-sectional area, A, fitted with a stopcock on top, is

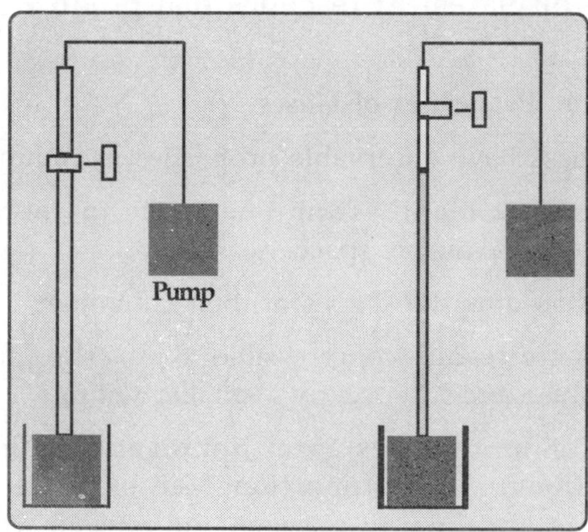

Fig. 3.1

inserted into the beaker so that the end of the tube is below the level of mercury in the beaker. Initially, the stopcock is open and the levels of mercury inside and outside the glass tube are the same. A vacuum pump is then attached to the top of the glass tube, and the air is pumped out. As this occurs, the mercury level rises in the tube until it reaches a height, h. Despite further pumping, the mercury level rises no higher in the tube. When all air has been pumped out of the tube, the stopcock is closed, and the mercury maintains its position in the tube. This behavior is understood as follows. Initially, before pumping, the atmosphere exerts the same pressure on the surfaces of mercury inside and outside the tube. Since $P_{out} = P_{in}$ = atmospheric pressure, the mercury levels inside and outside the tube are the same. As air is pumped out of the tube, its pressure on the mercury inside the tube decreases, and mercury rises in the tube to a height, h, such that the force due to the mass of mercury in the tube just counterbalances the pressure of the atmosphere on the mercury outside the tube. The height h is found to vary from day to day because the pressure of the atmosphere varies with weather conditions. However, its value is always in the neighborhood of 0.76 meters. For this reason, a unit of pressure called the atmosphere (atm) is defined as the pressure that will support a column of mercury 76 cm, or 760 mm, in height.

1 atm = 760 mm Hg

The pressure exerted by a column of mercury 1 mm in height is called a torr after Evangelista Torricelli, inventor of the barometer. Thus

1 atm = 760 mm Hg = 760 torr

In the English and SI systems, the units of pressure are respectively the pound per square inch and the pascal (1 Pascal = 1 Newton per square meter, where a Newton is the force required to accelerate a 1 kg body at 1 m/s^2). The pressure in Pa exerted by a column of mercury 760 mm in height can be readily calculated and will provide a conversion factor between SI and traditional non-SI units. The force exerted by a mass, m, of mercury is mg, where g is the acceleration due to gravity. This force is distributed over the cross sectional area, A, of the tube. The mercury therefore exerts the pressure, P = mg/A on the surface of mercury at the bottom of the tube. The mass of mercury can be calculated from its density, r, and its volume, which is Ah. Substituting for m in the expression for pressure gives equation 3-1-1:

[3-1-1): $P = \rho^*(Ah)g/A = \rho^*gh$

The pressure exerted by a column of mercury (or any liquid) of height h is independent of the cross sectional area of the column. The diameter of the barometer tube is therefore unimportant. Substituting the density of mercury (13.595 g/cm^3), the acceleration constant (g = 9.80665 m/s^2), and h = 0.760 m in 5-1-1 gives P = 1.0132 × 10^5 Nm^{-2} (1 Nm^{-2} = 1 Pascal). The following conversion relations are thus obtained:

1 atm = 14.7 lb/in^2 = 1.013 * 10^5 Pa (1 Pa = 1N/m^2)

= 1.013 bar (1 bar = 10^5 Pa)

Although the bar is official, the atmosphere and the torr are still the most commonly used pressure units in chemistry. We will therefore use the atm and the torr.

The pressure of a gas confined in a container cannot be measured with a barometer. For this a variety of devices may be used, the simplest being the manometer. A manometer is a U-shaped glass tube containing mercury or some less toxic fluid. The gas container is attached to one side of the manometer, and the other side is either open to the atmosphere (an open-end manometer), (*Fig. 3.2*) or evacuated (a closed-end manometer). The difference in the levels of fluid in the two arms of the manometer is a measure of the pressure of gas in the bulb through the relationship, $P_1 = P_2 + P$. Here P_1 is the pressure exerted by the gas on arm 1 of the manometer, P_2 is the pressure exerted on the arm of the manometer not connected to the gas container (arm 2), and P is the height of fluid in arm 2 minus the height in arm 1. P is positive if fluid is higher in arm 2 and negative if it is higher in arm 1. For an open-end manometer, P_2 is atmospheric pressure; for a closed-end manometer, P_2 is zero. If the manometer fluid is mercury, the pressure is in torr and may be converted to atm using the conversion factor given above. If the manometer contains some other fluid, the height of fluid may be converted to an equivalent height of mercury using the densities of the fluid and mercury.

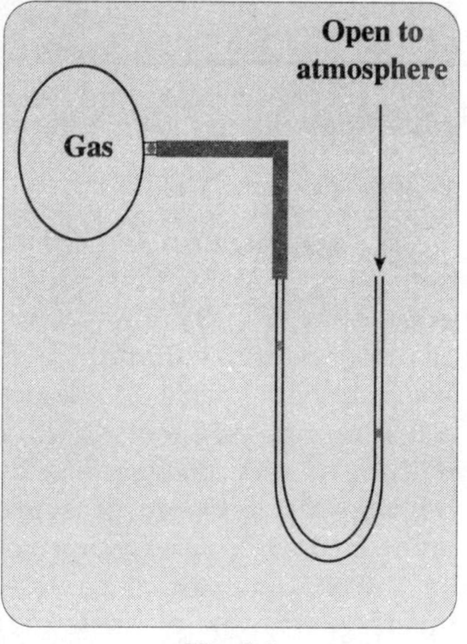

Fig. 3.2

The Ideal Gas Law

The ideal gas law is a relationship between the pressure (P), the volume (V), the amount (n), and the temperature (T) of a gas. It is presented in Eq. (3.1). The ideal gas law is called an equation of state, because it represents all possible states — combinations of P,V and T — in which the amount of gas, n, can be found.

$$PV = nRT \tag{3.1}$$

Where P is the pressure in atm; V is the volume in L; n is the amount of gas in moles, and T is the Kelvin temperature. R is a proportionality constant, remarkably the same for all gases, which relates the 4 variables..Eq. 3.1 is of simple form, which belies the effort expended in developing it. Over 200 years elapsed between the first quantitative experiments on gases and the final enunciation of Eq. 3.1. The simple form of the equation hides a remarkable sophistication in understanding. We now examine what the equation says regarding gas behavior.

Volume-Pressure Relation

If we rearrange the equation to solve for the volume, the equation states that volume decreases as the pressure exerted on (also by) the gas increases. The inverse relation of pressure and volume is a fact of every day experience. For example, when you compress the air in the chamber of a tire pump, you feel the increase in pressure of the air within. In 1662, Robert Boyle developed the quantitative relationship between pressure and volume that we now know as Boyle's Law, which states that the volume occupied by a fixed amount of gas at a fixed temperature varies inversely with the pressure exerted on the gas. Boyle's Law was the first-discovered component of equation 3 2-1. Note that the ideal gas law predicts that the volume should fall to 0 as pressure get s very large. For real gases this does not happen. At ordinary temperatures, most real gases will liquefy if pressure is made large enough. Once liquefication has occured, volume does not decrease much with increasing pressure. Real gases obey equation 3-2-1 closely only when P is not too large. This is why equation 3-2-1 is called the ideal gas law — it applies strictly only to an idealized gas, which does not liquefy but instead shrinks to zero volume when pressure is made very large.

Volume-Temperature Relation

The ideal gas law states that the volume occupied by an amount of gas, n, varies directly with the absolute temperature of the gas. A particular sample of gas, then, should double in volume if heated from 300 to 600 K. This behavior, too, is quite well known, at least qualitatively, in every day experience, as in the expansion (contraction) of a heated (cooled) balloon.

The relationship between gas volume and Celsius temperature was first established by Jacques Charles in 1800. He clearly established the linear relationship between the two quantities. Similar experiments relating gas pressure and temperature were carried out at about the same time by Gay-Lussac, and similar proportionality was found. In both cases, the relationships obtained were not so simple as the ideal gas law, because the absolute scale of temperature was not then recognized. The relation between volume and Celsius temperature is in Eq. 3.2.

$$V = \alpha^{*}t(^{\circ}C) + \beta \tag{3.2}$$

Plots of V versus t(°C) for gas samples containing different amounts of gas give different slopes and different intercepts on the V axis. However, they all give the same intercept on the t axis, -273.16 °C. This suggests that the zero of temperature be shifted 273.16° Celsius to the left. The resulting scale of temperature is, of course, the Kelvin scale. Eq. (3.2) takes the much simpler form, $V = \alpha^{*}T$.

A profound implication of Eq. (3.2) is that there exists a temperature at which the volume of gas should become zero. This temperature is called absolute zero. The Kelvin scale is set up so that 0 K corresponds to the temperature at which the volume of an ideal gas sample would become zero. This corresponds to -273.16 on the Celsius scale. Any temperature lower than this value would cause the gas to have negative volume. Since this is physically meaningless, the conclusion is that temperatures lower than absolute zero do not exist. That there is a lower limit on attainable temperature is not obvious from our everyday experience and from the manner in which we normally measure and think about temperature; the conclusion is nonetheless correct.

Relation Between Volume and Amount of Gas

The ideal gas law states that the volume occupied should increase in direct proportion with the amount (moles) of gas, when the gas is kept at the same pressure and temperature throughout. This is an extension of the hypothesis by Amadeo Avogadro in 1811 that equal volumes of different gases contain the same number of molecules. Avogadro made this statement in explanation of many observations about the relative volumes of gaseous elements that react to form compounds. It was in fact this hypothesis that finally allowed correct molecular formulas to be deduced and the atomic mass scale to be put on a firm basis.

The Value of the Gas Constant R

The gas constant R turns out to be an ubiquitous and extremely important quantity in physical science. We begin by obtaining a value for it based on the experimentally-measured volume of 1.0 mole of gas at 1.00 atm pressure and a temperature of 273.16 K. It is found that under these conditions the gas occupies a volume of 22.414 L. Rearranging Eq. (3.1) to solve for R, we can calculate its value:

$$R = PV/nT = (1.000 \text{ atm})(22.414 \text{ L})/(1.000 \text{ mole})(273.16\text{K})$$
$$= 0.08206 \text{ L-atm/K-mole}$$

The numerical value of R depends upon the units in which pressure and volume are expressed. P is commonly expressed in atmospheres or torr (both non-SI) or Pascal (SI), and V is commonly expressed in mL. Values of R in common P-V unit combinations are presented in Table 3.1.

From the Pascal-m^3 value, we see that R has units of energy/K-mole. It follows that the combined units L-bar, L-atm, and mL-torr are also energy units. We can express R in terms of any desired energy unit by using an appropriate conversion factor.

In using the ideal gas law, Eq. (3.1), the units of P, V, and R must be self-consistent, and the temperature must be expressed in Kelvins. A few examples of the use of the ideal gas law are now presented.

Table 3.1: R in Common Pressure-Volume Unit Systems

Pressure Unit	Volume Unit	R
atm	L	0.08206L-atm/K-mole
bar	L	0.08314 L-bar/K-mole
torr	mL	6.237 x 10^4mL-torr/K-mole
Pa	m^3	8.314 J/K-mole

Convert to the necessary units of T, P:

Initial	Final
T(K) = 273 + 19 = 292 K	T(K) = 273 K
P = 730 torr = 730/760 atm = 0.961atm	P = 1.00 atm
V = 326 mL = 0.326 L	V is unknown

Calculate the number of moles of gas under the initial conditions:

n = PV/RT = (0.961 atm)(0.326 L)/(0.08206 L-atm/K-mole) (292K) = 1.307 * 10-2 moles

Calculate volume at final T and P:

V = nRT/P = (1.307 * 10-2 moles)(0.08206 L-atm K-mole)(273K)/(1.00 atm) = 0.29 L (2 significant figures)

To shortcut this long process we take advantage of the constancy of the amount (moles) of gas. Since n is constant, PV/RT must also be constant, and its initial and final values are the same:

$P_iV_i/T_i = P_fV_f/T_f$

Solving for V_f and substituting numbers gives $V_f = 0.29$ L.

Dalton's Law of Partial Pressure

The ideal gas law can be applied to mixtures of gases as well as to single pure gases. Consider a mixture of two non-reacting gases, A and B, in a container of volume V. According to the ideal gas law, the pressure exerted by the mixture is given by Eq. (3.3).

$$P_T = n_T RT/V \tag{3.3}$$

Here n_T, the total moles of gas, is the sum of the moles of A and the moles of B:

$$n_T = n_A + n_B \tag{3.4}$$

Substitute Eq. (3.4) into Eq. (3.3) and expand:

$$P_T = (n_A + n_B)RT/V = n_A RT/V + n_B RT/V \tag{3.5}$$

Suppose that we could remove all of the molecules of B from the container. What pressure would A exert in the container alone? This is easily obtained from the ideal gas law to be PA = $n_a RT/V$. Similarly, $P_B = n_B RT/V$. Substituting the expressions for P_A and P_B into Eq. (3.5) gives Eq. (3.6).

$$P_T = P_A + P_B \tag{3.6}$$

This is Dalton's Law of partial pressures. In words, it says that the total pressure of a mixture of gases (P_T) is the sum of the partial pressures of the gases composing the mixture. The partial pressure of gas A is the pressure that n_A moles of A would exert if present alone in the container.

Dividing the expression for P_A by Eq. (3.6) gives Eq. (3.7).

$$P_A/P_T = n_A/n_T = n_A/(n_A + n_B) \tag{3.7}$$

The ratio of the moles of A to the total moles of all gases in the system is called the mole fraction of A, and is symbolized X_A. Thus $X_A = n_A/n_T$. Substituting this into Eq. (3.7) and rearranging, we obtain Eq. (3.8).

$$P_A = X_A P_T \tag{3.8}$$

The partial pressure of A in a mixture of A and other gases is the total pressure multiplied by the mole fraction of A.

Fig. 3.3 shows A and B, in a box. If the box has volume V, what fraction of this volume is occupied by A, and what fraction by B? A frequent answer might be that since half the molecules in the box are A, A occupies half the volume. This is, however, incorrect. If, when we fill the box with gas, we put A in first, the molecules of A will spread out to occupy the whole box. Now add some molecules of B. Since these molecules are "unaware" of the presence of A, they, too, will spread out in the entire volume. Thus both gases occupy the same volume — the entire volume of the container. VA = VB = V, the box volume. This is implicit in Eq. (3.3) and (3.5).

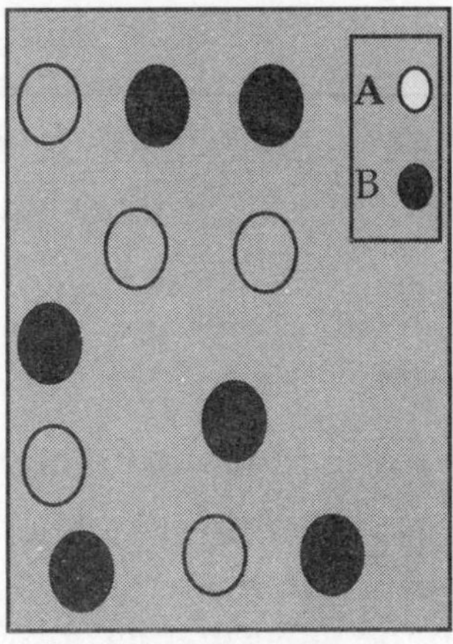

Fig. 3.3: **Dalton's Law of Partial Pressure**

Similarly, we assumed that temperature is the same for both gases: TA = TB = T. In contrast, the total moles, nT, is the sum of the moles of A and B; and the total pressure is the sum of the partial pressures. These relationships are summarized in Table 3.2.

Table 3.2: Relationships Among State Variables for a Gas Mixture

$T_A = T_B$	=	$T_{mixture}$
$n_A + n_B$	=	$n_{mixture}$
$P_A + P_B$	=	$P_{mixture}$
$V_A = V_B$	=	$V_{mixture}$

Dalton's Law is particularly useful in experimental situations involving the collection of gases over liquids. In such situations, the space above the liquid contains not only molecules of the gas, but also molecules of the vapor form of the liquid, produced by evaporation of the liquid. The vapor exerts a partial pressure that is part of the total pressure exerted by the gas mixture over the liquid. This partial pressure due to vapor that exists above the corresponding liquid phase is the vapor pressure, P_{vap}, of the liquid. According to Dalton's Law,

$$P_T = P_{gas} + (P_{vap}) \text{ liquid}$$

To calculate P_{gas}, we must correct the total pressure for the vapor pressure of the liquid, which we can look up in a table.

Kinetic Molecular Theory

The ideal gas law was developed from macroscopic observations, with no knowledge of the behavior of a gas at the molecular level. We now attempt to interpret the ideal gas law in terms of a reasonable molecular model (simple physical picture) of gas behaviour. What are the individual molecules doing, and why does their behavior manifest itself in the ideal gas law? We now enter the domain of theory — a mental interpretation of experimental results. The model of gas behavior currently accepted by scientists is the Kinetic Molecular model. The theory of gas behavior built on this model is called the Kinetic Molecular Theory (KMT). This theory is one of the oldest and most resoundingly successful in science.

First, we assume that gases consist of very small molecules. Since a gas occupies the entire volume of its container, and since gases readily diffuse, the molecules must move about in space. Consequently they have kinetic energy — energy of motion. Since gases are compressible, the molecules must be far apart. Focussing on an individual molecule, it seems reasonable to assume that it is a small particle that moves about at random, occasionally colliding with a wall of the container and with other gas molecules. The molecule sometimes gains and sometimes loses energy in these collisions, so that it frequently changes speed. Sometimes it moves rapidly, sometimes slowly. Thus our picture of the gas is dynamic rather than static.

These statements about gas molecules are consistent with the properties of gases listed at the beginning of the chapter. None of them have been proven, but they seem reasonable and constitute the postulates of the Kinetic Molecular Theory:

- Gases consist of molecules that behave like tiny hard spheres;
- The molecules have no volume — they may be treated as points;
- There are no forces of attraction between molecules;
- Collisions between molecules are elastic (kinetic energy is conserved);
- The molecules are in ceaseless random motion, frequently colliding with the container walls and with each other. A collection of gas molecules is highly disordered.
- The average kinetic energy of the molecules is proportional to Kelvin temperature.

We now pursue the consequences of these postulates. Postulate 6, the origin of which is not obvious, will be considered later.

Our aim is to develop an expression for pressure. At the molecular level, pressure must result from collisions of gas molecules with the container walls. A molecule hitting the wall exerts a force on it. The collection of all such forces on a unit area of wall during a given time interval constitutes the pressure. We should be able to calculate P from the force exerted by each collision, multiplied by the number of collisions per unit area of wall:

P = Force/Area = Force/collision x Collisions/area (3.9)

From Newton's second law, force is the rate of change of momentum. Thus

F = momentum change/time-collision x collisions/area

We move the time factor over to the second term to obtain Eq. (3.10).

F = momentum change/collision x collisions/ time-area. (3.10)

To obtain the momentum change per collision, envision a molecule moving directly toward a wall with velocity. Since momentum is conserved in any collision, the change in momentum of the molecule is:

momentum change = momentum after collision - momentum before

= m(-v) - m(v) = -2mv

The change of momentum of the wall must therefore be 2mv to give a total change of zero. We now have the first term in Eq. (3.10)

momentum change/collision = 2mv (3.11)

We take an intuitive approach to the second term. The number of collisions per unit time per unit area of wall should depend on (1) the number of molecules per unit volume in the container, N/V (the more there are, the more collisions there should be with the walls); and (2) the speed v at which a molecule moves (the faster the movement, the more collisions per unit time that should occur). Eq. (3.12) is based on these ideas:

collisions/time-area = (N/V)(v) (3.12)

If we assume for simplicity that the container is cubical, there are 6 walls over which these collisions must be spread. The collisions with a particular wall are then

collisions/time-area = Nv/6V (3.13)

(Despite our restrictive assumptions about the shape of the container, Eq. (3.13) turns out to be valid for a container of any shape!) We now multiply the expressions in Eq. (3.11) and Eq. (3.13) to obtain the pressure:

$$P = (2mv)(Nv/6V) = Nmv^2/3V \tag{3.14}$$

Rearrangment gives Eq. (3.15).

$$PV = Nmv^2/3 \tag{3.15}$$

This is as far as our molecular model takes us.

We are now at the interface between theory and experiment. Experiment (the ideal gas law) relates pressure and volume to temperature:

$$PV = nRT \tag{3.1}$$

Theory, Eq. (3.15), relates pressure and volume to the mass and speed of a gas molecule. To bring experiment and theory into correspondence, we must equate the right sides of the preceding two equations. In order for KMT to successfully explain the ideal gas law, it is necessary that

$$nRT = Nmv^2/3 \tag{3.16}$$

Equation (3.16) can be simplified by replacing n with N/N_o (No is Avogadro's Number); $mv^2/2$ by KE (the kinetic energy of an average gas molecule); and solving for KE. The result is

$$KEmolecule = 3RT/2No \tag{3.17}$$

Hence postulate 6! We refine this equation by making two further realizations. First, since R and N_o are both constants of nature, so must their ratio be. It is symbolized k, and is called Boltzmann's constant. Its value is 1.381×10^{-23} J/K-particle. Second, we have recognized that the kinetic energy of a gas molecule changes frequently as it undergoes collisions. However, its average speed over time is constant. The refined Eq. (3.18), is among the most important equations in science:

$$\text{Average } KE_{molecule} = 3kT/2 \tag{3.18}$$

The average kinetic energy of a gas molecule, no matter what its chemical identity, depends only on the Kelvin temperature. This gives a deep insight into the concept of temperature: it is a measure of the average kinetic energies of the molecules of a substance, hence a measure of their average speed. As T is increased, molecules move faster; as it is lowered, they move slower. The temperature at which molecular motion ceases is absolute zero. Temperatures lower than absolute zero are impossible because a molecule may not have negative kinetic energy.

Equation (3.18) is simple and profound. Is there an experiment that can be done to test its validity? There is in fact a simple experiment that verifies Eq. (3.18) in a rearranged form. If we replace the average kinetic energy of a molecule with the expression $m(v^2)_{avg}/2$, where $(v^2)_{avg}$ is the average of the square of the speed, and solve the resulting expression for $(v^2)_{avg}$, we obtain Eq. (3.19).

$$(v^2)_{avg} = 3kT/m \qquad (3.19)$$

The square root of $(v^2)_{avg}$ is called the root mean square speed, and is for our purposes approximately equal to the average molecular speed. Making this equality gives Eq. (3.20).

$$v_{avg} = (3kT/m)^{1/2} \qquad (3.20)$$

Multiplying both numerator and denominator of the argument on the right side of this equation by Avogadro's number No gives the useful variant in Eq. (3.21).

$$v_{avg} = (3RT/MM)^{1/2} \qquad (3.21)$$

The implication of Eq. (3.20) and Eq. (3.21) is that a heavy gas molecule moves more slowly than a light one, in a quantifiable way. The ratio of the speeds of the light (L) and heavy (H) molecules should be the square root of the inverse ratio of their molar masses:

$$(v_H/v_L)_{avg} = (MM_L/MM_H)^{1/2} \qquad (3.22)$$

In 1846, Thomas Graham measured the rates of diffusion of various gases. Diffusion is the process by which gases disperse in space via random molecular motion. The results of Graham's experiments are summarized in Eq. (3.23):

rate diffusion of gas A/rate of diffusion of gas B =
(density of gas B/density of gas A)1/2 (3.23)

The Maxwell-Boltzmann Distribution Law

We have said that in a gas the molecules move randomly, and that the speed of a molecule changes frequently. In the mid 1800's, James Clerk Maxwell in England, and Ludwig Boltzmann in Austria, were concerned with using statistical methods to describe, precisely and mathematically, the distribution of molecular speeds. The result of their efforts is called the Maxwell- Boltzmann Distribution Law. The curve is a plot of the fraction of molecules having speed *s*, f(s) (we use *s* for speed, *v* for velocity), versus the possible values of speed between zero and infinity. The curve has several noticeable features:

- The curve has the expected shape — low on both ends, indicating that few molecules have extremes of speed; and peaking in the middle, indicating that most molecules have speeds somewhere between the extremes.
- The curve is unsymmetrical because there is a definite lower limit (zero) but no definite upper limit to speed.
- The total area under the curve is the total number of gas molecules.
- The height of the curve at a particular speed (say s_1) is proportional to the fraction of molecules having speed s_1.
- The area under the curve between two speeds s_1 and s_2 (shaded in the figure) is the fraction of molecules haveing speeds in the range s_1 to s_2.
- The mathematical expression for f(s) obtained by Maxwell and Boltzmann is Eq. (3.24):

  $$f(s) = (\text{constant})(s^2) \exp(-ms^2/2kT) \quad (3.24)$$

  The s^2 term increases with increasing *s* and the exponential term decreases with increasing *s*. Thus f(s) first increases, but then peaks and decreases with increasing *s* as the exponential term takes over. The speed at the maximum of the curve, s_{mp}, is the most probable speed, because the greatest fraction of molecules have it.

- As T increases, the curve flattens and the maximum moves to higher speed, because the speeds of all molecules tend to increase with increasing T. The area under the curve stays constant, however, as long as the number of gas molecules is unchanged.

We now do two calculations using Eq. (3.24). First, we calculate the most probable speed, s_{mp}. This is a good approximation to the average speed, but the average will be somewhat larger because the curve is biased to higher speeds. s_{mp} is the speed at which f(s) is maximum. At this maximum, the slope of the plot — the derivative of f(s) — is zero:

$$df(s)/ds = d/ds\ [(s2)(\exp(-ms2/2kT))] = 0$$

$$= ds^2/ds\ \exp(-ms^2/2kT) + s^2\ d[\exp(-ms^2/2kT)]/ds = 0$$

$$= 2s\ \exp(-ms^2/2kT) - s^2(ms/kT)\exp(-ms^2/2kT) = 0$$

Dividing by the exponential, we obtain

$$2s - ms^3/kT = 0$$

This is readily solved for s_{mp}:

$$s_{mp} = (2kT/m)^{1/2}$$

As expected, this is a bit smaller than the root-mean-square speed in Eq. (3.20).

Next we calculate the average KE of a gas molecule by a method of averaging; we multiply each possible kinetic energy by the number of molecules with that kinetic energy, and divide by the total number of molecules. The required mathematical procedure is integration, as shown in Eq. (3.25).

$KE_{molecule}$ = Integral from 0 to Infinity of
$f(s)(ms^2/2)ds = 3kT/2$ (3.25)

Even if you are not yet able to carry out the integration, you should note that the result is the same as Eq. (3.18), which came from KMT. This is gratifying. It reinforces the validities of both KMT and the M-B Distribution Law.

Finally, we calculate the KE per mole of gas from the average $KE_{molecule}$:

$$KE_{mole} = N_o \times KE_{molecule}$$
$$= 3RT/2 \quad (3.26)$$

The kinetic energy of a mole of gas depends only on temperature. For this reason, kinetic energy of molecules is called thermal energy.

Summary of the Interpretation of the Ideal Gas Law in Terms of Molecular Behaviour

The relationship between the macroscopic and microscopic views of gas behavior can be summarized in several statements.

- Gases are compressible because they consist of small molecules that are far apart.
- Molecules of a gas are in constant motion, allowing gases to diffuse and to flow.
- Pressure results from collisions of gas molecules with the container walls.
- Pressure increases as volume decreases (Boyle's Law). A decrease in V increases the number of molecules per unit volume, leading to more molecular collisions with a unit area of the wall per unit time.
- An increase of temperature causes an increase in pressure (the Law of Gay-Lussac). KE of the molecules increases with T. Faster molecules cause an increase in pressure for two reasons:

- There are more collisions with the wall per unit time;
- Each collision exerts a greater force, since the molecule is moving faster.

- An increase in the amount (moles) of gas causes an increase in pressure at constant T (Avogadro's hypothesis). More gas means larger N/V. Higher N/V means more collisions per unit time and higher pressure.
- The ratio of diffusion rates of two gases is proportional to the square root of the inverse ratio of their molar masses (Graham's Law). This is a consequence of the average kinetic energy of a gas molecule being dependent only on T. At a particular T, a heavy molecule moves slower than a light one, but its larger mass offsets its smaller speed, giving the same kinetic energy. An important consequence of this is that a sample of gas with heavy molecules will exert the same pressure as a sample of gas with the same number of light molecules, as long as their temperatures and volumes are the same. Both samples satisfy the ideal gas law, independent of what their molecules are like. Although heavy molecules move slowly and strike the wall less often, they strike it with bigger mass, and cause the same pressure.

The Historical Role of Gas Phase Chemical Reactions

The first decade of the 19th century must have been both exhilarating and frustrating for chemists. On the one hand, Dalton's atomic theory (1803) rationalized many known facts about chemical elements, compounds, and reactions. In particular, the theory provided an explanation for the laws of conservation of mass, definite proportions, and multiple proportions, and gave a rational basis for the idea of reproducible combining masses of the elements in compound formation (e.g., the combining masses of oxygen and hydrogen in forming water are in the ratio 7.94 to 1). On the other hand, attempts to develop a scale of atomic masses were thwarted by the ignorance of chemical formulas. Chemists, led by Dalton, assumed that the formula for water was HO, and that water was formed from hydrogen and oxygen by Eq. (3.27):

$$H + O \rightarrow HO \tag{3.27}$$

This was the simplest assumption to make in the absence of definite knowledge of the formulas of elemental hydrogen, elemental oxygen, and water.

In 1809, Joseph Gay-Lussac conducted a series of experiments with gases that ultimately enabled the development of the atomic mass scale. Specifically, for reactions in which gases react to form other gases, he studied the relationships among the volumes of gaseous reactants consumed and the volumes of gaseous products formed. His result is of tremendous importance. Gay-Lussac discovered that, as long as the experiments were conducted at a constant temperature and pressure, the volumes of reactants used and products produced always gave whole-number ratios. One of many reactions that he studied was that between hydrogen and oxygen to form water vapor. He found consistently and reproducibly that for every one volume of oxygen used, two volumes of hydrogen were required, and two volumes of water vapor were produced:

$$\text{2 vol hydrogen} + \text{1 vol oxygen} \rightarrow \text{2 vol water vapour} \tag{3.28}$$

Gay-Lussac was not certain what to make of these results; however, Amadeo Avogadro was. He made the (to him) reasonable proposal that Gay-Lussac's results implied that equal volumes of gases, at the same temperature and pressure, contain equal numbers of molecules. In modern terms, we say that the volume occupied by a gas is proportional to the number of moles of gas present. Operating from this assumption, he concluded and stated that Dalton's view of the hydrogen/oxygen reaction, expressed in Eq. (3.27), was incorrect, because it was not consistent with the two-to-one-to-two hydrogen/oxygen/water volume ratios that Gay-Lussac observed. He then went on to propose that hydrogen and oxygen occur as diatomic molecules, and that water in fact contains two atoms of hydrogen per atom of oxygen, so that the water formation reaction becomes:

$$2H_2(g) + O_2(g) \rightarrow 2H_2O(g) \tag{3.29}$$

This is the simplest proposal consistent with the combining volumes observed; as we know today, it is entirely correct.

Gas Production via Double Displacement Reactions

It is appropriate in this chapter on gases to focus briefly on double displacement reactions that produce a gas as one of the products. An important series of examples of such reactions involves metal carbonate compounds (called carbonate salts) and acids as reactants. The reaction of a metal carbonate with an acid is shown generically in Eq. (3.30).

$$MCO_3(\text{s or aq}) + HX(aq) \rightarrow MX_2(aq) + H_2CO_3(aq) \tag{3.30}$$

This reaction does not have a gas as one of its products. However, in a subsequent step, carbonic acid, H_2CO_3, decomposes to water and carbon dioxide, a gas that escapes in part from the aqueous solution in the form of effervescence:

$$H_2CO_3(aq) \rightarrow H_2O + CO_2(g) \tag{3.31}$$

A specific example of the acid-carbonate reaction is shown in Eq. (3.32). Here the net reaction, obtained as the sum of Eq. (3.30) and Eq. (3.31) is shown.

$$Na_2CO_3 + 2\ HCl \rightarrow 2NaCl + H_2O + CO_2 \tag{3.32}$$

Acid-carbonate reactions are very important in at least two contexts. First, metal carbonates that have low solubility in water make up a substantial fraction of the earth's crust (limestone is an example). Deposits of carbonate rocks in contact with slightly acidic ground waters undergo reactions

Eq. (3.30) and Eq. (3.31). In so doing, they serve to maintain the acidity level of the water at a fairly constant level, supporting aquatic plant and animal life. Second, reactions Eq. (3.30) and Eq. (3.31) are important in the context of acid rain, which results when nitric acid, HNO_3, and sulfuric acid, H_2SO_4, are produced in the atmosphere from SO_2, produced in coal combustion, and NO_2, a byproduct of the internal combustion engine. Limestone (primarily calcium carbonate) is widely used in construction, and has been used for centuries as a medium for sculptors. Repeated and prolonged contact of building edifices and priceless works of art with acid rain results in their slow destruction as calcium carbonate reacts with nitric and sulfuric acids according to Eq. (3.30) and Eq. (3.31). Building edifices can be replaced; works of art cannot. Finally, dietary calcium tablets are made primarily of calcium carbonate. Contact of a stomach tablet with stomach acid (hydrochloric acid) causes the tablet to dissolve via reaction Eq. (3.33), after which the calcium can be utilized by the body.

$$CaCO_3(s) + HCl \rightarrow CaCl_2(aq) + H_2O + CO_2(g) \qquad (3.33)$$

Metal sulfites (for example, Na_2SO_3) react with acids in analogous fashion to form aqueous sulfurous acid, H_2SO_3. This subsequently decomposes to water and sulfur dioxide:

$$Na_2SO_3(aq) + HNO_3(aq) \rightarrow NaNO_3(aq) + H_2SO_3(aq) \qquad (3.34)$$

$$H_2SO_3(aq) \rightarrow H_2O + SO_2(g) \qquad (3.35)$$

4

Gas – Phase Ion Thermochemistry

The database concerned with ion thermochemistry makes available a reasonably complete listing of values for ionization energies.

- appearance energies
- electron affinities
- acidities
- proton affinities and gas phase basicities
- of molecules and molecular fragments

Data displayed for ionization energies, electron affinities and acidities are experimental values as reported in the literature, and are given along with a citation of the original paper; values for proton affinities and gas phase basicities are taken from a new re-evaluation of the relevant thermochemical scales. For the experimental data, guidance is provided (at least for the more common molecules) in the selection of a "best" value, when several different values have been reported for a quantity. Values for the gas phase enthalpies of formation of some of the common positive and negative ions derived from these data are displayed. The values for enthalpies of formation are presented using the so-called Ion Convention for treating the thermochemistry of the electron (rather than the Electron Convention commonly used in thermodynamics compilations).

In the August 1997 for the first time, the NIST Positive Ion (ionization energies, appearance energies), Proton Affinity (gas phase basicities, proton affinities) and Negative Ion (electron affinities, gas phase acidities) databases are combined into a single searchable Ion Energetics database. Because the Positive and Negative Ion databases were developed and maintained separately, the structures of the two sets of files are different, resulting in some inconsistencies in the way analogous data are presented in the WebBook. In future updates, these inconsistencies will be removed, but at the present time users should be aware that:

(a) data relevant to formation of positive ions are accessed through a search for the *precursor neutral species* while data on the thermochemistry of the anion is found by searching for the *anion*;

(b) when the box on the entry screen denoting a search for "Ion Energetics" data is checked, available data on gas phase basicities and proton affinities will be displayed with every "hit", while available data on gas phase acidities will not appear; in order to access gas phase acidity data, the user must also click on the box in the entry screen labeled "Reaction". For the same reason, the user will find that sometimes the same experimental technique is designated by two different acronyms in accessing results on positive and negative ions; because these acronyms are fully defined, it is hoped that this will not cause confusion.

Ionization Energy

The *ionization energy*, sometimes called (less correctly) the *ionization potential* (usually designated by IE, IP, or, in the older literature, I), is the energy required to remove an electron from a molecule or atom:

$$M \rightarrow M^+ + e^- \quad \Delta H_{rxn} = IEa$$

Ionization energies are characterized as adiabatic or vertical values.

Adiabatic Ionization Energy

The *adiabatic ionization energy* is the lowest energy required to effect the removal of an electron from a molecule or atom, and corresponds to the transition from the lowest electronic, vibrational and rotational level of the isolated molecule to the lowest electronic, vibrational and rotational level of the isolated ion. Adiabatic ionization energy data can be used to obtain values for the enthalpy of formation of the ion, M^+.

Vertical Ionization Energy

The *vertical ionization energy* is the energy change corresponding to an ionization reaction leading to formation of the ion in a configuration which is the same as that of the equilibrium geometry of the ground state neutral molecule. According to the Franck-Condon principle, when a molecule is ionized by photoionization or by interaction with energetic electrons, the highest probability configuration of the resulting ion will be the configuration of the precursor neutral molecule. When the equilibrium geometry of the ion is very similar to that of the neutral precursor molecule, the vertical and adiabatic ionization energies will be the same, or nearly so. The vertical ionization energy must always be greater than or equal to the adiabatic ionization energy.

Appearance Energy

Since ionization energies are often determined in experiments in which the ionizing photon or electron energy is varied until the appearance of an ion is observed ("threshold measurements"), ionization energies have sometimes been called appearance energies. However, in general usage this term has come to have a more specific meaning. As used here, and in most of the technical literature, the term *appearance energy*, sometimes (less correctly) called the *appearance potential*, refers to the minimum energy required to form a particular fragment ion from a precursor neutral molecule:

$$AB \rightarrow A^{+} + B + e^{-} \ \Delta H_{rxn} = AP$$

For more information see the description of the presentation of appearance energy data, the discussion of the use of appearance energy data to derive enthalpies of formation of fragment ions, as well as the description of some of the complicating factors involved in the interpretation of appearance energy data.

Proton Affinity and Gas Phase Basicity

Stable cations formed in the gas phase also include protonated neutral molecules, generated in proton transfer reactions. Formally, the relationship between the enthalpy of formation of MH+ and its neutral counterpart, M, is defined in terms of a quantity called the *proton affinity*, PA. This the negative of the enthalpy change of the hypothetical protonation reaction:

$$M + H^{+} \rightarrow MH^{+} \ \Delta H_{rxn} = -PA$$

$$\Delta_f H^{o}(MH^{+}) = \Delta_f H^{o}(M) + \Delta_f H^{o}(H^{+}) - PA$$

The term proton affinity, as universally used, is a quantity defined at a finite temperature, usually 298 K, and is therefore not strictly analogous to the adiabatic ionization energy or electron affinity, both of which are the 0 K enthalpy changes of the corresponding reactions.

At 298 K, the enthalpy of formation of the proton, using the Ion Convention (or "stationary electron" convention), is 365.7 kcal/mol, 1530.0 kJ/mol.

The Gibbs energy change associated with the protonation reaction is called the *gas phase basicity*, GB, of molecule M. Most available data on gas phase basicities and proton affinities has been obtained from experiments in which the equilibrium constants of proton transfer reactions are determined. See the discussion of derivation of thermochemical data from ion/molecule equilibrium constants for relevant equations and details.

Electron Affinity

The *electron affinity*, EA, of a molecule is, for negative ions or anions, the quantity that is analogous to the ionization energy for positive ions. That is, the electron affinity is equal to the energy difference between the enthalpy of formation of a neutral species and the enthalpy of formation of the negative ion of the same structure. The electron affinity is defined as the negative of the 0 K enthalpy change for the electron attachment reaction:

$$M + e^- \rightarrow M^- \ \Delta H_{rxn} = -EAa$$

$$-EA = \Delta_f H^\circ(M^-) - \Delta_f H^\circ(M) - \Delta_f H^\circ(e^-)$$

As with the ionization energy, it is possible to have either vertical or adiabatic electron affinities, with the numeric value of the vertical quantity being greater than or equal to the adiabatic value. A difference from the ionization energy is that for stable ("bound") negative ions, the ion is lower in energy than the corresponding neutral. If the negative ion is higher in energy than the neutral, the neutral is said to have a negative electron affinity, and the ion will undergo spontaneous loss of the electron.

Gas Phase Acidity and Relative Acidity

The *gas phase acidity* (or merely, *acidity*) of a molecule AH, Δ_{acid} G(AH), is the Gibbs energy change of the reaction:

$$AH \rightarrow A^- + H^+$$

usually defined at 298 K. The enthalpy change of this reaction, $\Delta_{acid}H$, is, of course, the proton affinity of the anion. The Gibbs energy change of the reaction:

$$AH + B^- \rightarrow BH + A^-$$

is called the *relative acidity* of species AH and BH. Most data are derived from determinations of the equilibrium constant of this reaction. See the discussion of derivation of thermochemical data from ion/molecule equilibrium constants for relevant equations and details.

Enthalpies of Formation of Ions in the Gas Phase

The *enthalpy of formation (or heat of formation) of an ion in the gas phase* can, in principle, be obtained through a straightforward treatment of the thermochemistry of the ionization process. For example, the enthalpy of formation of a positive molecular ion is obtained by adding the enthalpy of formation of the precursor molecule to the adiabatic ionization energy (IE) and subtracting the enthalpy of formation of the electron.

$$\Delta_f H^o(M^+) = \Delta_f H^o(M) + IE_a - D_f H^o(e^-)$$

while that of an anion is based on the analogous quantities combined with the value for the electron affinity:

$$\Delta_f H^o(M^-) = \Delta_f H^o(M) - EA + \Delta_f H^o(e^-)$$

Similarly, enthalpies of formation of positive *fragment ions*, A^+, are given by:

$$\Delta_f H^o(A^+) = \Delta_f H^o(AB) - \Delta_f H^o(B) - \Delta_f H^o(e^-) + AP$$

assuming that there is no potential barrier in the reaction coordinate for the dissociation reaction, and little or no kinetic shift.

Note that in the equations given here, there is no reference to temperature, but in practice, one may have to be concerned about the fact that the ionization energy or electron affinity is a quantity corresponding to a zero degrees Kelvin process, while the available data on the enthalpy of formation of the neutral species may correspond to some higher temperature. This presents a complication (especially for those interested in highly accurate data) in the derivation of enthalpies of formation of ions in the gas phase. A rigorous treatment of enthalpies of formation of ions at finite temperatures requires a consideration of the changes in the ionization energy/enthalpy of formation with temperature. However, when high accuracy is not required, the simplifying assumption that the adiabatic ionization energy is approximately equivalent to the 298 K enthalpy of ionization is usually adequate. (For a more detailed presentation, see the discussion of the thermochemistry of ions in the gas phase at finite temperatures.)

In this compilation, the Ion Convention for treating the thermochemistry of the electron is used. This essentially means that the terms involving the electron can be ignored in these equations.

Thermochemical Conventions for Enthalpies of Formation of Ions

In order to derive enthalpies of formation of positive or negative ions in the gas phase using ionization or appearance energy data, it is necessary to treat the thermochemistry of the electron. There are two conventions, both in widespread use, for dealing with the thermochemistry of the electron, one (the *Ion Convention*) used by the ion chemistry/physics community, and one (the *Electron Convention*) used by thermodynamicists.

The Ion Convention

According to the "*Ion Convention*" (sometimes unfortunately called the "stationary electron convention") which is adopted here, the enthalpy of formation of the electron at non-zero temperatures is equal to the integrated heat capacity of the electron; when data are treated this way, the enthalpy of formation of the electron cancels out in calculating the enthalpy of formation of an ion. That is, in this convention, which is adopted by most mass spectrometrists and other ion physicists and chemists, the thermochemistry of the electron can be ignored when deriving an ion enthalpy of formation.

The Electron Convention

Thermodynamicists commonly use the "*Electron Convention*" which treats the electron as a *standard chemical element* with an enthalpy of formation defined as zero at all temperatures. Since standard thermodynamics is a non-rationalized system, the effect of constraining the enthalpy of formation of the electron gas to zero at all temperatures, is that the electron's integrated heat capacity must be accommodated elsewhere in the equation — namely, in the derived value for the enthalpy of formation of the ion. Therefore, in standard thermodynamics data compilations, cited values for enthalpies of formation of ions at temperatures other than 0K differ from those given here. Because in standard thermodynamic data compilations, the integrated heat capacity of an electron gas has commonly been taken to be the same as that of an ideal gas following Boltzmann statistics - 5/2 RT — a value for an "Ion Convention" enthalpy of formation of a positive ion is numerically more negative than the value in the "Electron Convention" by 5/2 RT (6.2 kJ/mol at 298 K); that for a negative ion, is more positive by the same amount.

History, Coverage, and Presentation of the Database

History

The collection of gas phase ion energetics data traces its origin to a series of publications concerned with this subject area, beginning with a table of ionization energies and evaluated enthalpies of formation of ions included in the 1957 book "Electron Impact Phenomena and the Properties of

Gaseous Ions" by F. H. Field and J. L. Franklin In 1969, H. M. Rosenstock and collaborators, from the National Bureau of Standards, joined Field and Franklin to expand that table in the publication "Ionization Potentials, Appearance Potentials, and Heats of Formation of Gaseous Positive Ions" In 1977, H.M. Rosenstock, K. Draxl, B.W. Steiner, and J.T.Herron published an update, "Energetics of Gaseous Ions," which included a complete re-evaluation of the data, and for the first time, a table of electron affinity data.

In 1982, an extensive compilation of ionization potential and appearance potential data, "Ionization Potential and Appearance Potential Measurements, 1971-1981", presented unevaluated measurements which had appeared in the literature from the 1971 cut-off date of the previous collection up to mid-1981. In 1988, an evaluation or re-evaluation of the data from the collective database presented in all these earlier publications, was published in "Gas-phase Ion and Neutral Thermochemistry" (commonly referred to as "the GIANT Tables"). The 1988 publication also included more recent data and evaluated proton affinity values, as well as a comprehensive table of data on negative ions, including both electron affinity and gas phase acidity values. The data on proton affinities were taken from a 1984 publication in which the entire thermochemical scale of gas phase basicities and proton affinities had been evaluated.

The 1988 publication of evaluated data on ion thermochemistry was made available by the National Institute of Standards and Technology's Standard Reference Data program as a searchable computer database available on diskettes — in fact, as two jointly-distributed databases, one presenting the data relevant to positive ions and the other, data on negative ions . In the initial release, the negative ion database displayed the entire corpus of data from which the evaluations were drawn, but the original version of the electronic database on positive ions presented only evaluated values for ionization energies, proton affinities, and enthalpies of formation of positive ions in the gas phase. The 1991 and 1993 updates to the electronic database added more recent data, and, in the case of the positive ion collection for the first time displayed some of the original data (e.g. data published after 1971) from which the evaluations were drawn.

After new experimental determinations had made necessary a re-evaluation of the entire proton affinity scale as presented in the 1984 publication (data derived from equilibrium constant determinations are interdependent and must be evaluated collectively), proton affinity data which had appeared in the original electronic database were removed from the updated version to prevent dissemination of out-of-date information. The re-evaluation of the proton affinity scale has now been completed and the evaluated proton affinity and gas basicity data are included in the WebBook.

Coverage

The ion energetics database at the present time has as its focus numeric data concerned with the energies for formation of particular positive and negative ions in the gas phase, as well as with the energetics of certain reactions, namely protonation and deprotonation, of those ions. That is, the database includes values for ionization energies, appearance energies, electron affinities, gas phase acidities and basicities, as well as proton affinities. In addition, the database contains data on the energies associated with the clustering of neutral molecules to anions.

Thermochemical information about positively-charged ion/molecule clusters has been compiled. Some information on ionization energies of small cluster ions (with not more than three or four ligand molecules), especially in inorganic systems, is included. The database does not at the present time include thermochemical data derived from collisionally-activated dissociation experiments of positive ions, although such results for negative ions are included.

A particular explanation about the coverage of ionization energy data is in order. In most of the precursor publications the primary focus was the thermochemistry of ions in the gas phase. That is, the goal of collecting ionization energies, appearance energies, electron affinities, and so forth was the derivation of enthalpies of formation of ions. Because of this emphasis, the coverage of data was restricted to information directly relevant to deriving ionic enthalpies of formation. This limited focus had particular implications for the coverage of data on ionization energies, since it necessarily meant that only data on the lowest ionization energies was included; ionization energies leading to the formation of excited ions, or multiply charged ions were excluded (except for atoms and diatomic molecules in the 1977 publication Furthermore, coverage was restricted to adiabatic ionization energy data except in cases where publications gave only vertical ionization energy values. In abstracting data from the more recent literature (since 1993), we have attempted to include both adiabatic and vertical values where both are available, but have not gone back to the thousands of earlier papers to re-abstract data on vertical ionization energies or upper ionization energies that were not originally included.

Presentation

The positive ion database (ionization energies, appearance energies, proton affinities) and negative ion database (electron affinities, acidities) were developed and are maintained separately. As a result, certain inconsistencies exist at the present time in the presentation of the two types of data in the Web Book. For example, the primary sort in the anion database depends on the identity of the anion, while the positive ion database has always been organized around the identity of the precursor neutral molecule. For this reason, until further work has been accomplished, users of the WebBook will occasionally see an apparently illogical list of "hits" when data for a particular chemical species has been requested.

For example, when carrying out a sort for "ion energetics" data, if the database contains both ionization/ appearance energy data and electron affinity data for species M, then M will be listed twice in the list of "hits", once as M (giving data on the energies associated with ionization of M to M+) and once as M- (with data on the electron affinity of molecule M). Retrieval of data listed under M will also lead to a table giving the proton affinity and gas phase basicity of molecule M, if they are available. Unlike gas phase basicity data, data on gas phase acidities can be retrieved only if you started the search by requesting data on "reactions" (in addition to "ion energetics") on the opening screen. The gas phase basicity/proton affinity data are, at the present time, presented in less detail.

The formal organization of the positive and negative ion data based on neutral precursor (positive ions) or on the ion also has implications for carrying out a search for data based on registry number. For positive ion data, searches should be conducted based on the registry number of the neutral species; for anion data searches should be conducted on the registry number of the anion. Since the database contains registry number data for a limited portion of the anions in the database, a chemical formula search will often be a better choice for finding a specific anion.

Appearance energy data are presented in two ways. First, by calling up all data for a particular molecule, you access a listing of all ionization energy determinations, and also the appearance energies that have been determined for fragmentation processes of that parent ion. Second, if you are interested in knowing the appearance energies determined for the formation of a particular ion through fragmentation of larger species, you are given the option (at the top of the display) to "View reactions leading to ____+ (ion structure unspecified)". By clicking on this text, you will access a list of all appearance energies determined for formation of fragment ions of that particular formula from other (larger) molecular species. It should be understood that in the great majority of cases, the structure of the fragment ion is not specified, and such data should be used mainly as auxiliary information, or as a guide to the original literature. However, in some cases where the original authors have carried out a sufficient analysis to be able to specify the structure of the fragment ion, this structure is indicated. (In other cases, the structure may be obvious, and such an indication is not necessary.) A word of caution is in order: again, in earlier versions of the database, such specifications were not included, and we have not yet gone back to fill in this missing information.

Units

Units used for the display of information are dictated by the current practices for reporting data of a particular kind. For example, ionization energy and electron affinity values are usually reported in electron volts, and that is the unit used here for these data. The user is given the option of displaying values for enthalpies of formation of ions, proton affinities, and gas phase basicities in kJ/mol or kcal/mol, both of which are widely used in the relevant literature.

The conversion factors which were used are: 1 electron volt (eV) = 23.06054 kcal/mol = 96.4853 kJ/mol; 1 kcal/mol = 4.184 kJ/mol, as given by the 1986 CODATA compilation.

Thermochemical Conventions for the Electron

The enthalpy of formation of any chemical species is defined as the difference between the enthalpy of the compound and the sum of the enthalpies of the elements of which it is composed. However, in the case of an ion, M^+ or M^-, one must explicitly take into account the enthalpy of the electron in some way. There are two widely-used conventions for dealing with the thermochemistry of the electron, one—called the "Electron Convention"—used predominantly by thermodynamicists and one—"the Ion Convention"—commonly adopted by scientists studying ion physics/chemistry. The "Ion Convention" is used here.

There is considerable confusion and misunderstanding of the basic assumptions and treatment of the thermochemistry of the electron in the two approaches. In fact, the so-called "electron" and "ion" conventions are really names assigned by the ion chemistry community to the two different conventions used by thermodynamicists for handling the integrated heat capacity of elements. The more widely-used convention (corresponding to the "electron convention") defines the enthalpies of formation of elements in their standard states to be zero at all temperatures; in this case, the integrated heat capacity of the element must be accommodated elsewhere in any thermodynamic equation, as shown in the more detailed discussion below — and in the particular case in which we are interested (ionization) end up as an increment in the derived enthalpy of formation of the ion. There is also a community of scientists in Europe (SGTE) who define the enthalpy of formation of elements at temperatures above absolute zero to be equal to the integrated heat capacity of the species; this corresponds to the treatment used for the electron in the so-called "ion convention". As will be derived below, when this treatment is followed, the integrated heat capacity term cancels out in the expression defining the enthalpy of formation of the ion. Of course, enthalpies of reaction are identical when using the two conventions (provided the same value is chosen for the integrated heat capacity term in question); the value of the integrated heat capacity merely appears on opposite sides of the equation, with opposite signs.

Further confusion exists because in the past, users of the two conventions have cited different values for the integrated heat capacity of the electron: Standard thermodynamics works usually using the "electron convention", have taken a value of 5/2 RT (6.197 kJ/mol at

298 K), that is, the heat capacity of an ideal gas under Boltzmann statistics. Ion chemists/physicists, in deriving values for enthalpies of formation of ions, have in much of the earlier literature stated that they were assuming a value of zero for the integrated heat capacity of the electron; since the term cancels out in deriving an ion heat of formation in the "ion convention", the value chosen was, in fact, moot. A correct treatment of the heat capacity of an electron gas uses Fermi-Dirac, rather than Boltzmann, statistics A 1994 publication arrives at a value of 3.145 kJ/mol (0.033 eV) for the integrated heat capacity of an electron gas at 298 K, and is recommended for use in instances (such as reactions where the electron appears as a reactant) where the term does not cancel out.

Because of these differences in the treatment of the thermochemistry of the electron, values for the gas phase enthalpies of formation of ions at temperatures other than absolute zero cited in standard thermochemical compilations differ from those given here or in most mass spectrometric literature, usually by 5/2 RT (6.197 kJ/mol at 298 K). Values for enthalpies of formation under the Electron Convention are higher (more positive) for positive ions and lower (less positive) for negative ions than the corresponding values expressed in the Ion Convention. Problems arise when users unknowingly mix inconsistent values for enthalpies of formation in the same equation. The Table lists several commonly-used compilations and shows which convention is used in each.

INTERPRETATION OF ION THERMOCHEMISTRY DATA

This section provides brief descriptions of some of the factors relevant to the interpretation and evaluation of ionization energy and appearance energy data. More detailed discussions of the ionization process are available in many books and reviews, notably in the Introduction to "Energetics of Gaseous Ions" Material presented here has as its focus those aspects of the subject which have a bearing on the evaluation of data on ionization energies, appearance energies, or ion/molecule equilibrium constants.

Ionization Thresholds

The Franck-Condon Principle

Ionization of a molecule by photoionization or by energetic electrons (sometimes called "electron impact") is governed by the Franck-Condon principle, which states that the most probable ionizing transition will be that in which the positions and momenta of the nuclei are unchanged. Thus, when the equilibrium geometries of an ion and its corresponding neutral species are closely similar, the energy dependence of the onset of ionization will be a sharp step function leading to the ion vibrational ground state. However, when the equilibrium geometry of the ion involves a significant change in one or more bond lengths/angles from that of the neutral species, the transition to the lowest vibrational level of the ion is no longer the most intense, and the maximum transition probability (the vertical ionization energy) will favor population of a higher vibrational level of the ion; if the geometry change is great, it is possible that the transition to the lowest vibrational level of the ion (i.e. the adiabatic ionization energy) will not even be observed.

A sharp onset indicates that the equilibrium geometries of ion and neutral are quite similar, and that photoionization or electron impact determinations of the ionization threshold are likely to be free of complications. When an ionization process proceeds according to the second situation pictured in the figure, the onset of the photoelectron band is observed approximately at the adiabatic ionization energy; adiabatic ionization energies derived from observation of the onsets of photoelectron bands are usually in excellent agreement with adiabatic ionization energies obtained from optical spectroscopy (analyses of Rydberg series) or from the most reliable threshold determinations.

When the equilibrium geometry of the ion is very different from that of the corresponding neutral molecule and the lowest vibrational level is not populated in ionization by photon absorption or electron ionization, it has been shown that values for the adiabatic ionization energies can be obtained by determining the equilibrium constant for charge transfer to another molecule of known ionization energy:

$$A^+ + B \leftrightarrow B^+ + A$$

In such determinations, the ions are at thermal equilibrium with their surroundings, and one measures the thermochemical properties of the ions in their equilibrium geometries. The enthalpy change for this reaction, which is obtained from the equilibrium constant determination, is just the difference between the enthalpies of ionization, $?H_I$, of species A and B. As derived in the discussion of thermochemistry of ions at finite temperatures, this difference is likely to be quite close to the difference in the adiabatic ionization energies:

$$\Delta H = [\Delta H_I (B) - \Delta H_I (A)] \sim [IE_a (B) - IE_a (A)]$$

This, in part may be due to a problem described as pertaining to accurate determination of the reactive neutral pressure in pulsed high pressure mass spectrometers. The pressure in the source of such an instrument has often been in the transition regime between molecular and viscous flow. This can cause appreciable fractionation of neutral species in the bath gas, based on the diffusivity of the compound, which is related to the square root of the mass. Thus, both relative and absolute neutral pressures may have been poorly characterized in such experiments in the past. These could vary from instrument to instrument, based on design, and from experiment to experiment, based on varying operating conditions. Other possible contributing factors are clustering of neutral molecules to the ions at low temperatures, and pyrolysis of the ions at high temperatures.

Therefore, at the present time, it appears that the most reliable values for entropy changes associated with such ion-molecule equilibria can be obtained by judiciously examining experimentally-determined entropy changes in conjunction with ab initio calculations of those quantities.

Thermochemical scales derived from equilibrium constant determinations are, of course, scales of *relative* thermochemical values. Absolute values for thermochemical quantities can be assigned if a reliable value for the quantity in question (ionization energy, electron affinity, proton affinity, acidity, etc.) is available for one or more species in the scale.

The evaluation of thermochemical scales derived from equilibrium constant determinations presents special challenges, since the data for different molecules are all interrelated, so the scale must be evaluated as a whole, not molecule-by-molecule. That is, evaluation of such a thermochemical scale imposes the requirements of internal consistency in three parameters, ΔG (at different temperatures), ΔH and ΔS; furthermore, final absolute values assigned for properties of individual compounds must be consistent with what is known about enthalpies of formation of the relevant species, or with entropies of reaction that would be predicted from statistical mechanics and values (when available) of absolute entropies of the relevant species. In addition, trends in data for homologous series or compounds of a particular structural type must make sense.

The major uncertainty in data derived from equilibrium constant determinations, aside from the question of whether thermodynamic equilibrium is actually attained, is in knowing the temperature accurately. In the recent re-evaluation of the extensive scales of proton affinity and gas basicity, it was found that for the large body of data evaluated in the 1984 publication the thermochemical scales (particularly the end of the scale representing high gas phase basicities) had been significantly constricted because operating temperatures of the instruments used in the experiments had been underestimated. For this reason, users will find that certain cited values for proton affinities and gas basicities given here are significantly different from those listed earlier although for all species for which sufficient information was available to do a complete evaluation, internal consistency is maintained.

Most ion/molecule equilibrium studies have been devoted to the derivation of extensive scales of relative proton affinities and gas phase acidities. The results were mainly derived from interlocking ladders of enthalpy changes for the proton transfer reactions:

$$AH^+ + B \leftrightarrow BH^+ + A$$

$$AH + B^- \leftrightarrow A^- + BH$$

Other published ion/molecule equilibrium studies provide data on charge transfer:

$$A^+ + B \leftrightarrow B^+ + A$$

$$A^- + B \leftrightarrow B^- + A$$

which yield scales of relative enthalpies of ionization or electron affinity at finite temperatures. A thermochemical ladder of relative ionization energies determined in this way closely reproduces the equivalent scale of spectroscopic ionization energies, thus demonstrating the reliability of the approach for deriving information on relative ionization energies.

The most useful application of this approach for ionization energy data has proved to be the determination of ionization energies for species which undergo a large change of geometry upon ionization, and which therefore exhibit very gradual onsets of ionization as a function of energy. For example, the only reliable information about the adiabatic ionization energies of n-alkanes and of alkyl hydrazines comes from thermochemical ladders established through equilibrium constant deter-minations. Since the electron transfer occurs in a long-lived collision complex which endures for many vibrational periods, the ionic configuration corresponding to the equilibrium geometry of the ion (the geometry corresponding to the adiabatic transition) is accessed.

Other equilibrium studies have been concerned with hydride or halide transfer reactions:

$$R_1^+ + R_2X \leftrightarrow R_2^+ + R_1X$$

(where X is H, F, Cl, Br, or I). Studies of hydride transfer and halide transfer equilibria have led to quantitative information about the relative enthalpies of formation of alkyl carbocations. These data were used to supplement information from appearance potential determinations in evaluating enthalpies of formation of alkyl carbocations.

EXPERIMENTAL TECHNIQUES

In this section, we summarize briefly the different types of experiments from which the data presented here originate, and where possible indicate the strengths and/or limitations of the different techniques, and how these influence the evaluator in arriving at a recommended value for a particular property.

In the database, techniques are identified by acronyms, shown in square brackets in the discussion, or in some cases, after the appropriate headings. A problem in defining an experimental technique for the purposes of assigning acronyms in the database is that acronyms used in the literature have evolved over the years as experimental techniques evolve, so that for a collection like this one with experimental results originating over a 70-year time period, a problem of internal consistency arises. Because of this problem, we have elected to use fewer, more broadly-defined acronyms, rather than attempt to maintain a detailed breakdown of experimental techniques, which may differ only in subtle details, in the assignment of acronyms. Even using broadly-defined acronyms, there are certain studies for which it is difficult to pigeonhole the experimental technique; for example, the borderline between "photoionization" and "laser spectroscopy" is sometimes not easily defined, and the distinction is sometimes made more on the basis of the focus of the study than on the actual details of the experiments.

For at least two specialized techniques that would logically fit under our broad umbrella-acronyms, we have assigned individualized acronyms, because the data provided by these techniques— time-resolved photodissociation (TRPI) which is actually a photoionization (PI) technique, and photoion-photoelectron coincidence (PIPECO)—which could also be considered either photoionization (PI) or a threshold electron detection (TE) technique – are uniquely informative. In the case of time-resolved photodissociation results, measured appearance energies often differ significantly from those determined using other techniques since slow fragmentation processes are detected.

Optical Spectroscopy(S)

The identification of a Rydberg series in an atomic or molecular spectrum leads to a value for the ionization energy. In cases where the analysis of the spectrum is straightforward, the spectroscopic ionization energy values are highly accurate. The determination of atomic ionization energies through optical spectroscopy is a highly developed field which has been extensively reviewed. A large fraction of atomic ionization energies listed here are from expert evaluations of atomic spectra. In the evaluation of ionization energies of atoms and diatomic molecules, spectroscopic ionization energies have been chosen as "selected values" where they are available. For polyatomic species, a value derived from an analysis of the optical spectrum has been given great weight, unless several determinations from other highly reliable techniques are in conflict with the spectroscopic value.

Threshold Experiments

The most widely-used technique for determination of ionization and appearance energies involves a direct determination of the minimum energy required to form a parent or fragment ion from a neutral species, or to detach an electron from a negative ion. In these approaches, ionization may be effected by photoionization, by interaction with energetic electrons ("electron ionization" or, in older literature, "electron impact"), or by interaction with excited atoms (Penning ionization) or other chemi-ionization reactions; the measurement involves a determination of the minimum energy ("threshold") required to form an ion. The resulting ions or the ejected electrons, or both, are detected using various mass spectrometric techniques.

Electron Ionization Techniques (EI), (EIAE)

Over the years, the most widely-used techniques for the determination of ionization and appearance energies have involved the use of mass spectrometers in which ionization is effected by an electron beam. The energy of the beam is varied, and the abundance of the resulting ion(s) is monitored; the "onset" of the ion on the energy scale must be detected. A problem with this approach that had to be dealt with before accurate data could be obtained was that standard electron beams had a large energy spread, so the nominal energy expected from the applied electrode potentials was not a good indication of the actual energy of electrons in the beam. However, by the 1960s, techniques were developed to narrow the energy range of the electron beams through the use of so-called "electron monochromators", in which the energy of the electron beam is narrowly defined by passing the beam through electron energy selectors of various designs. Other laboratories have utilized a so-called fast-beam apparatus to determine accurate ionization cross sections as a function of electron energy. Modern results obtained using electron beams with well-defined energies are in excellent agreement with analogous results derived from determinations of photoionization thresholds.

Some electron ionization data reported here were never intended to be accurate ionization energy/appearance energy determinations, but were carried out simply as diagnostic measurements, to unravel chemical processes occurring in particular systems (such as in the vapor over a Knudsen cell).

All of these techniques are simply designated by the acronym "EI" or for negative ions "EIAE". Measurements made using the more careful approaches can be distinguished from the non-quantitative measurements by the cited error limits or (where there are no error limits given) by the number of significant figures displayed. Most of the quantitative measurements made during the past 20 years have been made with well-defined electron energies.

Photoionization Techniques

Photoionization Mass Spectrometry (PI), (PD), (LPD)

In the mid-1960s, the problem of exactly defining the energy of the ionizing agent was approached in some laboratories by replacing the electron beam by photons, whose energy could be well defined. In classical photoionization mass spectrometry, monochromators were used with standard light sources, and the ion abundance was determined as a function of photon energy. That is, the approach to determining a threshold energy was exactly analogous to that used in electron ionization experiments. In such experiments, as with the electron ionization techniques, one must be able to detect the onset of ionization. According to the Franck-Condon Principle, if the configuration of the ion is different from that of the precursor neutral molecule, the *onset* of ionization as a function of energy will be gradual, and the exact onset may be difficult to pinpoint accurately.

Modern photoionization experiments often utilize laser or synchrotron light sources, and may have other distinctive features designed to provide more detailed information. For example, studies are published examining pressure- or time-dependencies of ionic photodissociation processes. The latter are assigned a separate acronym here (TRPI), rather than being categorized with other "photoionization" experiments, since observed onsets may differ markedly from onsets measured on the conventional time-scale, and it is useful to be able to recognize (through the acronym) why this is so.

The electron affinity of a species can be determined by finding the threshold for electron photodetachment, via irradiation of a trapped negative ion by variable frequency light. This is denoted by the acronyms [PD] for photodetachment, using a continuous frequency light source and a monochromator, or [LPD] for use of a variable frequency laser as the light source.

Time-Resolved Photodissociation (TRPD)

Two complementary photoionization methods are often used for studying dissociation processes where a "kinetic shift" exists (that is, where experimentally-observed ionization onsets are higher than the thermodynamic onset energy due to the fact that the apparatus samples the fragmenting ions at a certain time when ions undergoing a slow fragmentation process have not yet had time to dissociate). These approaches, both of which examine the dissociation process as a function of time, are time-resolved photodissociation (the acronym TRPD is used in the literature) and time-resolved photoionization mass spectrometry (the acronym TPIMS is used in the literature). In time-resolved photodissociation experiments, parent ions are formed by electron impact, thermalized, and photoexcited by a monochromatic pulsed laser; the dissociation is followed as a function of time in an ion cyclotron resonance spectrometer (ICR). In time-resolved photoionization mass spectrometry, ions are formed by a pulsed VUV light source in an ion trap, and are ejected after a given delay time into a quadrupole mass filter. While both approaches give time-resolved information about dissociation processes, they are complementary rather than effectively the same since in the former technique, all parent ions are excited to the same energy, while in the latter, parent ions are excited to a range of internal energies extending from zero up to the maximum available energy.

Laser Spectroscopy (LS)

Spectroscopic studies using laser techniques have provided highly accurate ionization energy values. For example, ionization energies for molecules have been determined using multiphoton ionization or resonance-enhanced multiphoton ionization (REMPI) of vibrationally-cooled species in a molecular beam. In these studies, the cooled beam of molecules is raised to a specific excited state by irradiation with a tunable laser; while this excitation energy is held constant, a second independently tunable laser is used to ionize the beam of excited molecules, with the photon energy being tuned through the ionization onset. The excitation laser is then tuned to a different transition, and the ionization scan is repeated. In this way, the entire Franck-Condon accessible region of the intermediate electronic state is mapped out, insuring that the molecular geometry corresponding to the adiabatic ionization energy is accessed. Since every intermediate vibronic state leads to an independent value of the ionization threshold, the experiment contains an internal consistency check.

For atoms, the related technique known as Resonance Ionization Mass Spectrometry (RIMS) is sometimes employed to determine accurate ionization energies.

Photoelectron Spectroscopy (PE), (LPES)

It is also ossible to determine the energy change associated with an ionization process by effecting ionization with a photon of well-defined energy and measuring the energy of the ejected electrons:

$$M + h\upsilon \rightarrow M^{+} + e^{-}$$

where

$$KE(e^{-}) = h\upsilon - I - E^{*}(vib, rot)$$

(where E^{*} (vib, rot) is the internal energy of M+ and I is the binding energy of the electron).

The most widely-used technique of this type is conventional photoelectron spectroscopy in which the photon sources are usually the helium or neon resonance lines (21.218 eV and 40.813 eV or 16.848 eV and 16.671 eV, respectively) or other intense monochromatic sources. In such an experiment, the ejected electrons will have differing energies depending on the distribution of energy levels in the M+ ions formed; a map of the abundances of the ejected electrons as a function of energy is called the photoelectron spectrum. The shapes of the photoelectron bands will reflect not only the energy differences in the different states of M^{+}, but also show the $M \rightarrow M^{+}$ transition probabilities as governed by the Franck-Condon principle. In cases where the equilibrium geometry of the ion and the corresponding neutral are the same or are similar, it is found that the observed onset of the first photoelectron band is usually a reliable indicator of the adiabatic ionization energy. This situation is easily recognized by the sharp onset of the photoelectron band.

Most photoelectron spectroscopy studies are carried out with the goal of elucidating the *spectroscopy* of the system through determinations of vertical ionization energies leading to the ground state and excited state ions, and therefore, little attention is usually given to determinations of adiabatic ionization energy values. In many instances, figures showing the photoelectron spectra are displayed, and onsets of photoelectron curves which correspond approximately to the adiabatic ionization energies can be estimated from the figure. Such values are reported here, but are surrounded by parentheses to indicate that these are approximate values not selected by the original authors.

For negative ions, if a beam of ions is irradiated by a laser beam with photons in excess of the energy required to detach the electron, then analysis of the translational energy of the detached electrons allows for determination of the electron affinity. This technique [LPES] can provide electron affinities precise to micro-electron volts. The method often provides information on the vibrational states of the neutral and ionic species as well. However, the assignment of the (0-0) threshold can be complicated by these states. The precision is commonly better than 0.2 kJ/mol, and can be much better.

Threshold Electron Detection

Highly accurate determinations of ionization energies come from a family of techniques in which laser ionization (e.g. REMPI) or pulsed field (PFI) techniques are combined with the detection of energy-selected electrons. In so-called "threshold photoelectron spectroscopy" or "zero-kinetic energy spectroscopy" (the acronym "ZEKE" is often used in the literature) ions with a well-defined energy are formed, and only those electrons which correspond to essentially zero energy of ejection are detected. Such experiments yield vibrationally/rotationally resolved spectra of the ions. In some cases, mass analysis of the positive ion is included (mass-ZEKE). The acronym [ZEKE] is used in the negative ion data base here.

Photoion-Photoelectron Coincidence Spectroscopy

For the purposes of studying the thermochemistry of ionic fragmentation processes, a powerful variation of the Threshold Electron Detection approach is used which involves the simultaneous detection of a (single) zero-kinetic energy electron and the corresponding (single) positive ion. In the technique known as photoion-photoelectron coincidence (or sometimes, photoelectron-photoion coincidence—PEPICO), ejected electrons which originated with "zero" kinetic energy are matched with their corresponding positive ions. At energies where parent ions, M+, are undergoing dissociation to form one or more fragment ions, one obtains the relative probabilities for the formation of the daughter ions from parent ions of exactly known energy (i.e. the breakdown curve). The ions can be detected at differing times after the ionization event for the determination of the time dependence of the dissociation process. The complete interpretation of such data requires a modeling of the dissociation using statistical theories of unimolecular decomposition (i.e. quasi-equilibrium/RRKM theory), but the thermochemistry and detailed mechanism of an ionic fragmentation process can be mapped out very accurately. As pointed out by Dannacher in spite of its great strengths, this technique has not been widely utilized, possibly because of the intricate instrumentation required, the complexity of the data analysis, and the fact that each determination requires the investment of a great amount of time on the part of the experimentalist.

Chemi-Ionization [CI]

In the older literature, Penning Ionization — ionization by collisions with a beam of metastable neutral rare gas atoms with known excitation energy or energies — was often used as an ionization mechanism.

$$X^* + M \rightarrow M^+ + X + e^-$$

In these experiments, metastable atoms employed include mixtures of He(2^3S) (19.818 eV) and He(2^1S) (20.614 eV), Ne($^3P2$) (16.619 eV) and Ne($^3P0$) (16.715 eV), or Ar($^3P2$) (11.548 eV) and Ar($^3P0$) (11.723 eV). Because of the presence of two metastable states in a given atom beam, the Penning electron spectrum consists of a shifted superposition of two spectra, each formed by one of the species. The energy of the ejected electrons was analyzed.

Some recent studies have examined systems where other chemi-ionization reactions such as:

$M + X_2 \rightarrow MX^+ + X^-$

occur, and have obtained thermochemical data from experiments in which the collision energy is varied, and positive and negative product ions are counted and analyzed mass spectrometrically.

Charge Exchange Mass Spectrometry [CEMS]

In this technique, ionization is effected through charge exchange:

$X^+ + M \rightarrow M^+ + X$

and a determination of the absolute cross section for production of M^+. A series of charge donors, X^+, of varying recombination energies (that is, where the ionization energy of X varies) are used. The plot of cross section as a function of recombination energy provides values for ionization and appearance energies. Because a continuous energy scale is not available with this technique, error limits are usually of the order of ±0.1 eV.

Neutral Beam Ionization or Appearance Energy [NBIAE], [NBAE]

Collision of a neutral species with an energetic particle of low ionization potential, such as an alkali atom, can result in electron transfer, giving an alkali cation and an anion. The electron affinity of the neutral species is equal to the translational energy of the alkali atom less its ionization energy. Deter-minations of electron affinities by this method have the advantage that one obtains values for the true electron affinity: electron attachment to a neutral species, rather than detachment from an anion. Certain anions can be produced by this technique which are not accessible via electron impact due to low energy exit channels, e.g. CCl_4 Due to the limited energy resolution of the neutral alkali beam, the precision of this technique is not high, typically 20 kJ/mol. The onset energies of fragment ions can also provide useful thermochemical information, if the thermochemistry of the coproduced neutral species is known. Normally this technique results in a determination of the adiabatic electron affinity, but for a sufficiently fast beam of neutral species, the onset corresponds to the vertical attachment energy of the electron, which, in contrast to detachment methods, is smaller than the adiabatic value.

Electric Field Detachment [EFD]

Negative ions with electron affinities of a few tenths of an electron volt or less can undergo detachment of the electron in a strong electric field. Based on the strength of the field, the dipole moment of the neutral species produced, and the rate of loss of the electron, the electron affinity can be derived. This often is used to access information on negative ions where the electron is in a non-valence state, such as dipole-bound anions.

Thermochemical Information from Studies of Ion/Molecule Reactions

Ion/Molecule Equilibrium Constant Determinations [EQ], [IMRE], [TDEq], [TDAs]

An ion/molecule equilibrium:

$$A^+ + B \leftrightarrow C^+ + D$$

$$A^- + B \leftrightarrow C^- + D$$

is established in a high pressure mass spectrometer, flow tube, or ion cyclotron resonance spectrometer, and the equilibrium constant is determined by observing the relative abundances of the two ions, $A^{+/-}$ and $C^{+/-}$ after a large number of collisions:

$$K_{eq} = [C^{+/-}]\,[D] \;/\; [A^{+/-}]\,[B]$$

(where $A^{+/-}$ and $C^{+/-}$ are generic representations of positive/ negative ions). The neutral reactants, B and D, are present in great abundance compared to the ionic reactants, and therefore, the ratio [D]/[B] does not change as equilibrium is established. A single measurement leads to a value for the Gibbs energy change of reaction at the temperature of the measurement, while a series of measurements at different temperatures permits an experimental evaluation of the entropy and enthalpy changes associated with the reaction:

$$- RT\ln K_{eq} = \Delta G^o = \Delta H^o - T\Delta S^o$$

The main uncertainty associated with this technique, aside from the necessity of ensuring that the system is at a true thermodynamic equilibrium, is that the temperature of the reacting system must be accurately known. Although the reproduction of relative spectroscopic ionization energies through equilibrium measurements carried out in widely different pressure regimes demonstrates that this is not a serious problem, it is true that the initially-reported networks of gas phase basicities led to thermochemical ladders that were constricted by as much as 15% because of problems with temperature determinations In addition, since the measurement leads only to *relative* thermochemical data, the resulting thermochemical ladders must be related to reliable comparison standards if absolute values are desired.

In the negative ion database, the acronym [IMRE] is used to indicate an equilibrium measurement made at a single temperature, while [TDEq] denotes those at multiple temperatures. [TDAs], for temperature-dependent association, is used in specific case of association equilibria such as:

$$A^- + B \leftrightarrow AB^-$$

The positive ion database uses the identifier [EQ] for all such results.

Determinations of Reaction Endothermicity [END], [Endo]

Some thermochemical data reported here comes from studies where the enthalpy change of an endothermic ion/ molecule reaction is determined. Information about the thermochemistry of a particular ion is obtained when relevant thermochemical data for other species participating in the reaction is available. In a very few instances, such information comes from straightforward kinetic treatments (Arrhenius plots) of the temperature dependencies of the rate constants of endothermic ion/molecule reactions. However, more commonly a so-called guided-beam apparatus is utilized for such determinations. Ions are generated in a flow tube, extracted and mass analyzed, then focused at the desired kinetic energy into a static cell containing the neutral reactant. The kinetic energy of the reactant ions is varied, and reaction onsets are determined as a function of translational energy.

Ion/Molecule Bracketing Experiments [IMB], [IMRB]

There are some ion/molecule systems for which an equilibrium can not be established in an ion source, either because one of the relevant neutral species is unstable (e.g. a radical or unstable molecule) or because of competing reactions in the system. In such cases, it is sometimes possible to obtain an experimental estimate of the enthalpy change of a particular reaction (charge transfer, proton transfer, hydride transfer, etc.) by use of a technique known as "bracketing" in which the ion of interest is reacted with a series of molecules chosen for variations in the relevant thermochemical parameter (ionization energy, electron affinity, gas phase basicity, acidity). The occurrence, and sometimes the rate constant, of reaction is monitored as a function of the parameter of interest. The approach is based on the assumption that an endothermic reaction will not be observed, or will occur only at a low efficiency. Thus, the approximate onset energy is usually assumed to lie on the energy scale at a point where the rate of reaction becomes very slow. One problem with this approach is that the reaction of interest may be exothermic (even highly exothermic) but will not be observed if another, more favorable reaction channel is available to the reacting pair.

In the positive ion database, only a few gas phase basicity values are derived from such measurements, but the information from these experiments is useful in evaluating conflicting experimental results from other techniques. More widespread use of this technique is made in the negative ion database.

The Kinetic Method [KIN], [BRAN]

If certain criteria of similarity in structure occur, the ratio of ions from the competitive fragmentation of an dimeric ion has been shown to reflect the thermochemical stability of the product ions. The energy for activation of the precursor ion can be from collision-induced dissociation, chemical activation, or the ion may be formed is a metastable state. Proton-bound species such as $MeNH_3^{+}\cdots H_2NEt$ or $MeOH\cdots{}^{-}OEt$ are examples of the structures applicable to this method. A calibration line based on the ion ratios of several species with energetics known from other methods, such as ion/molecule equilibria, is necessary to assign quantitative values in this experiment. Values denoted as [BRAN] for negative ions are from chemically-activated species; those labeled [BRAN] (positive ions) or [CIDC] (negative ions) are from metastable or collisionally-activated species.

The Electron Capture Detector [ECD]

An electron capture detector, using a beta source, can be modified to operate in a time resolved mode. By modeling the response of the ECD as a function of both time and temperature, the rate constants for both attachment and detachment of electrons can be determined, and thus the equilibrium constant for binding the electron can be obtained, leading to a value for the electron affinity. The method appears limited to EAs of 1 eV or so and less.

The Electron Swarm [ES]

The rate constant for electron attachment to a neutral can be measured as a function of mean electron energy in a drift tube. When combined with detachment rate constants from a beam technique, the electron affinity can be estimated. This gives a lower limit, which is often up to 0.5 eV too low.

Other Experimental Techniques

Essentially all of data included in this collection have been derived from results obtained using the experimental approaches listed above. Data are also included which result from the use of several additional techniques that are not easily placed in the broad categories as organized here.

Charge Inversion Energy Loss Spectrometry [*CIEL*]

Positive ions are generated by an electron beam and accelerated to translational energies well above thermal (4-6 eV), mass-selected and transmitted into a collision-gas cell, where they undergo collisions with an appropriate target gas. Electron capture reactions with the target molecules occur:

$$M^+ + T \rightarrow M + T^+$$

$$M + T \rightarrow M^- + T^+$$

Any stable anions that are formed are translational-energy analyzed prior to detection. As only forward-scattered anions are detected, the translational energy losses associated with these species are essentially equal to the endoergicities of their formative process.

Collisionally-Activated Dissociation [*CAD*], [*CIDT*]

Ions are generated, mass selected and accelerated into a chamber where they collide energetically with target molecules, and undergo collisionally-activated dissociation processes. The onset energies for particular dissociations are determined. Most of the body of data originating from this type of experiment has not been incorporated into the positive ion database, in that the quantity which is determined is the energy required to form a fragment ion from a precursor *ion* (rather than from a neutral species), and therefore, to match conventions used for presenting data in this database, the collisional onsets must be normalized by adding them to the appropriate ionization energy. In the future, this body of data will be re-examined, and, if there is sufficient demand, will be incorporated into an auxiliary database. There is extensive use of this method in the negative ion database, where the acronym [CIDT] is used.

Delayed Thermionic Ionization [*DTI*]

The one study using this technique whose results are included in the database was an investigation of fullerenes. Ions and neutral molecules in the gas phase were generated by laser desorption from stainless steel target rods coated with C_{60} or C_{60} /C_{70} films. Delayed ionization by thermionic emission during the flight time between source and time-of-flight acceleration optics was detected by withdrawing ions perpendicular to the cluster beam. Thermionization rates were determined from these measurements, and ionization energies were derived from the results using statistical mechanical formulations. For details, users are referred to the original reference.

Charge Transfer Spectra [*CTS*]

The charge transfer spectrum method is a semi-empirical method often used, especially in the past, to estimate ionization energies of large molecules such as polycyclic aromatics and certain biochemical compounds. It is based on a semi-empirical theory developed by Mulliken to explain the absorption bands of electron donor-electron acceptor complexes in solution. These bands arise from a transition from the ground state of the molecular complex to an excited state in which an electron is largely transferred from the donor to the acceptor molecule. The bands are not characteristic of the isolated donor or acceptor molecules. Hastings et al derived from the Mulliken theory a simple algebraic relation between the frequency of the maximum of the charge transfer band and the ionization energy of the donor, and correlated it with experimental information. A limited comparison of ionization energies derived by this method and more accurate methods indicates that the estimates are usually within a few tenths of an electron volt of the more correct value.

Auger Electron Spectroscopy [*AUG*]

The technique of Auger Electron Spectroscopy is similar in principle to photoelectron spectroscopy. It is based on an analysis of the energies of ejected electrons. However, in this case the electron is ejected via an Auger cascade following prior inner shell ionization. The inner shell ionization is brought about by a high energy electron beam or a discrete X-ray source.

Surface ionization [*SI*]

The surface ionization method has been applied to the determination of first ionization energies of some metal atoms. The method is based on the assumption that the atoms in a beam, after impinging on a hot metal surface, will come to thermodynamic equilibrium, producing a surface concentration of atoms and ions whose composition can be described by the Saha-Langmuir equation:

$$N_+/N_0 = g_+/g_0 \exp[e(f - I)/kT$$

where N_+/N_0 is the fraction of the atoms which are ionized, g_+ and g_0 are the statistical weights of the ions and atoms, e is the electronic charge, f the work function of the metal, I the ionization energy, k the Boltzmann constant, and T the absolute temperature. The temperature dependence of the positive ion current gives the ionization energy if the work function is known. Complications include the effect of surface coverage or impurities on the work function, definition of the work function for a polycrystalline surface exhibiting a variety of crystal planes with different work functions, and an occasional lack of reproducibility of experimental results. Where comparisons can be made with more reliable methods, determinations of relative ionization energies using this approach reproduce other results within several tenths of an electron volt.

For negative ions, a common version of this experiment, the Magnetron technique, lacks mass analysis, and therefore many of the values for thermochemical parameters resulting from this method correspond to anions of uncertain identity. Precision is claimed to be several tenths of a volt (>20 kJ/mol), but appears to be worse in many cases, based on current data.

Liquid-Phase Electrochemical Determinations [*LE*]

Several studies have been published in which gas phase ionization energies are determined from measurements of photocurrent thresholds of compounds dissolved in nonpolar solvents. This approach was used primarily for obtaining ionization energy data for non-volatile organic compounds. The Born equation is employed to obtain the solvation energies for the cations.

Electron Auto-Detachment Rate [*KINT*]

For negative ions with electron affinities of less than about 0.5 eV, the rate for auto-detachment of the electron as a function of temperature can be measured. The activation energy obtained from this represents the electron affinity.

Electron Transmission Spectroscopy [*ETS*]

In this technique, the scattering of a monoenergetic electron beam impacting on a gas at less than the ionization threshold is determined. The presence of resonances in the spectrum implies electron capture to produce a temporary state, followed by autodetachment. This is the principal technique for measurement of negative electron affinities, i.e. cases where the anion is less stable that the neutral species. Occasionally, a series of resonances can be extrapolated to below zero electron energy to give an estimate of a positive electron affinity.

Kinetic Mobility of Ions [*MobI*]

If the mobility of an ion in a gas can be measured in response to a weak electric field, the potential well depth, corresponding to the enthalpy for the ion associating with the neutral gas can be determined.

Laser Optogalvanic Spectroscopy [*LOG*]

The gas of interest is subjected to an electrical discharge, and the discharge region is probed by a laser. The 'LOG' spectrum is recorded by scanning the wavelength of the laser, and monitoring laser-induced changes in the discharge impedance. The spectrum produced will be similar to the laser absorption spectrum but relative intensities of spectral features may be very different. The method is particularly suitable for detecting unstable (radical) species.

Zero-pressure Thermal-radiation Induced Dissociation [*ZTID*]

In an Paul (ICR) trap, infrared radiation from the walls is absorbed by trapped ions. If a weak bond exists in the ion, the ion can dissociate to a new ion and neutral species, as its internal energy increases with time. Modelling of the rate constant for this process can yield a bond strength.

Scattering of Atoms from Ions [*Scat*]

If a beam of ions is passed through a gas of some neutral species, and the resulting ion-neutral complex both has an appreciable binding energy, and undergoes electron loss in this process, then an electron affinity for that complex can be derived from the scattering as a function of translational energy of the ion beam.

Non-Experimental Methods

Derivation [DER]

In a number of instances, authors have derived values for ionization energies or appearance energies through a variety of approaches. The most common type of derivation is based simply on taking the difference in enthalpies of formation of an ion and its corresponding neutral species, usually when for some reason an ionization energy can not be directly determined, but the necessary enthalpy of formation values are available from other measurements. This is not the only type of derivation appearing in the literature, however; results cited here include a variety of other types of derivation.

***Estimation* [*EST*]**

In a few instances, results have been included that are designated as "estimated." The chief difference between a "derived" value and an "estimated" value is that derived values are usually closely tied to specific experimental results related to a particular ion, while "estimated" results usually come from an examination of trends in data for a series of molecules. Such results have been included here only when they come from studies that are sufficiently careful and systematic that the results appear to have some value for users searching for information about a particular ionic species. For both "derived" and "estimated" results, interested users should consult the original references for details.

***Evaluation* [*EVAL*]**

Literature covered in putting together the database included reviews and papers where the authors have carried out expert evaluations of particular systems. Values recommended by the authors of such publications are included here and are specifically noted as "evaluations" by using the acronym EVAL.

***Calculations* [*Calc*]**

The present work is intended to be an experimentally-based compilation. At present, only for the IE and EA of the hydrogen atom do calculations rival and even surpass the accuracy of experimental work.

***Lattice Energy Calculations* [*Latt*]**

The heat of formation of an anion can be derived from a Born-Haber cycle using the lattice energy and heat of formation of a crystal and the thermochemistry of the appropriate gas phase cation. This method is not especially accurate relative to more recent techniques, but for some singly charged inorganic anions it provides the only data available.

RELIABILITY OF DATA AND CRITERIA FOR EVALUATION

Comparisons Among Results of Different Techniques

The ion energetics data are derived from the various different methods described above, and are consequently of widely varying quality, not only because the accuracies of the measurement techniques differ, but also because of differences in the focuses of the research in which the measurements were made. For example, many of the ionization energies reported for inorganic species were never intended by the original authors to be quantitative ionization energy measurement, but are simply qualitative indicators of whether or not a given ion observed in the vapor over a heated Knudsen cell has been formed by electron impact ionization of the corresponding neutral species (in which case it exhibits an onset at a relatively low energy) or through fragmentation of a molecular ion (which would correspond to a higher onset energy). In these experiments, error limits of ±0.5 to l eV are commonly cited by the original authors.

In carrying out an evaluation of data to arrive at a recommended value for an ionization energy, an attempt is made to integrate the entire corpus of information about any given ion, giving weight to various determinations depending on the nature of the ionization onset, the measurement techniques used, the attention to detail by the original authors, and so forth. For atoms or diatomic molecules, a spectroscopically-determined ionization energy is usually (but not always) considered more reliable than a contradictory value obtained by observation of an ionization threshold. Data obtained from coincidence experiments and other highly accurate measurements based on laser spectroscopy techniques are usually considered to be the most reliable. A value obtained from an observed ionization onset using photoionization or electron ionization with well-defined electron energies is considered more reliable than an onset obtained using less accurate techniques. In all of these cases, an observed onset of a photoelectron band is given great weight in carrying out the analysis, with values from simple onset observations being downgraded if they do not match the photoelectron onset (unless, of course, the differences could be rationalized in terms of the principles outlined above).

As mentioned above, many photoelectron spectroscopy studies do not cite values for adiabatic ionization energies. In cases where the authors have provided a figure showing the photoelectron spectrum, it is sometimes possible to estimate from the figure the value for the adiabatic onset; where listed adiabatic ionization energies have been obtained in this way, the values are shown surrounded by parentheses, and should be considered to be only rough estimates.

Most of the proton affinity data have been derived from ion/molecule equilibrium constant determinations. The values reported here are taken from the recent re-evaluation of proton affinity data, and differ somewhat from those listed in the frequently-cited 1984 evaluation, since the scale of relative values of proton affinities was shown to have been constricted, and has now been expanded in agreement with recent results and calculations. Other equilibrium constant data have been utilized as an aid in evaluating information obtained from other sources.

Error Limits

The experimentally-determined data collected here display widely varying uncertainties, ranging from ±0.0001 eV or smaller for some optical- or laser-spectroscopic determinations to ±l eV for electron ionization measurements carried out on the vapour above a heated Knudsen cell. When the original authors do not indicate error limits, no limits are listed here. Some of the ionization energy values are shown enclosed in parentheses. These indicate data which were not reported in the original paper, but which have been derived by us from a figure or other information in the paper.

In some cases, a recommended value for an ionization energy is given. Recommended values may originate from an analysis of the original experimental data listed for the species; in this case, cited error limits are derived from the various experimentally-determined values for the ionization energy using standard statistical analyses of the data. As explained above, different weights are given to determinations, depending on the accuracy of the experimental technique used; in most cases, this means that when measurements derived from reliable techniques are available, those that are clearly unreliable (for example, an ionization onset determination made with an electron beam where the energy spread of the electrons is broad) are disregarded. In a few cases, recommended values come from reviews in which the authors have carried out detailed data evaluations; when those evaluations are accepted for this database, the value reported in the review is listed, with "EVAL" (evaluation) given as the technique, and that value, with its error limits, is simply reproduced in the space for our recommended value.

5

Gas Chromatography

In gas chromatography (GC), the stationary phase is a high-boiling liquid and the mobile phase is an inert gas. In the organic chemistry teaching labs at CU Boulder, GC is used as an analytical tool to find out how many components are in a mixture. It can also be used to separate small amounts of material.

The GC Instrument

The process of gas chromatography is carried out in a specially designed instrument. A very small amount of liquid mixture is injected into the instrument and is volatilized in a hot injection chamber. Then, it is swept by a stream of inert carrier gas through a heated column which contains the stationary, high-boiling liquid. As the mixture travels through this column, its components go back and forth at different rates between the gas phase and dissolution in the high-boiling liquid, and thus separate into pure components. Just before each compound exits the instrument, it passes through a detector. When the detector "sees" a compound, it sends an electronic message to the recorder, which responds by printing a peak on a piece of paper.

The GC consists of an injection block, a column, and a detector. An inert gas flows through the system. The injection chamber is a heated cavity which serves to volatilize the compounds. The sample is injected by syringe into this chamber through a port which is covered by a rubber septum. Once inside, the sample becomes vaporized and is carried out of the chamber and onto the column by the carrier gas.

The carrier gas is an inert gas, helium. The flow rate of the gas influences how fast a compound will travel through the column; the faster the flowrate, the lower the retention time. Generally, the flow rate is held constant throughout a run. (The GCs at CU Boulder are set at a flow rate of 55 mL/min.)

In a professional laboratory, the GC conditions would be critical for another experimenter trying to duplicate your observations. All of our GCs have the same columns (1.5% OV-101 on Chromasorb G) and the same flow rate (55 mL/minute) and detector bridge current (150 mAmps). Each instrument will have a different setting for:

- column temperature
- injection port temperature
- detector temperature

It is a good practice to write down some of the settings on the instrument. The values for these temperaturs are viewed by turning the knob on the instrument below the gauge.

Recorders

Two devices are used to record the GC traces/areas under peaks:

- integrating recorders;

- computer programme.

Each type of device records the messages sent to them by the detector as peaks, calculates the retention time, and calculates the area under each peak; all of this information is included in the printout. For similar compounds, the area under a GC peak is roughly proportional to the amount of compound injected. If a two-component mixture gives relative areas of 75:25, you may conclude that the mixture contains approximately 75% of one component and 25% of the other.

Retention Time (RT)

The retention time, RT, is the time it takes for a compound to travel from the injection port to the detector; it is reported in minutes on our GCs. The retention time is measured by the recorder as the time between the moment you press start and the time the detector sees a peak. If you do not press start at the same time you inject your sample, the RT values will not be consistent from run to run.

Factors which Affect GC Separations

Efficient separation of compounds in GC is dependent on the compounds traveling through the column at different rates. The rate at which a compound travels through a particular GC system depends on the factors listed below:

- **Volatility of compound**: Low boiling (volatile) components will travel faster through the column than will high boiling components.
- **Polarity of compounds**: Polar compounds will move more slowly, especially if the column is polar.
- **Column temperature**: Raising the column temperature speeds up all the compounds in a mixture.
- **Column packing polarity**: Usually, all compounds will move slower on polar columns, but polar compounds will show a larger effect.

- **Flow rate of the gas** through the column: Speeding up the carrier gas flow increases the speed with which all compounds move through the column.
- **Length of the column**: The longer the column, the longer it will take all compounds to elute.. Longer columns are employed to obtain better separation.

Generally the number one factor to consider in separation of compounds on the GCs in the teaching labs is the boiling points of the different components. Differences in polarity of the compounds is only important if you are separating a mixture of compounds which have widely different polarities. Column temperature, the polarity of the column, flow rate, and length of a column are constant in GC runs in the Organic Chemistry Teaching Labs. For each planned GC experiment, these factors have been optimized to separate your compounds and the instrument set up by the staff.

CHROMATOGRAPHY

Chromatography is the collective term for a family of laboratory techniques for the separation of mixtures. It involves passing a mixture dissolved in a "mobile phase" through a *stationary phase*, which separates the analyte to be measured from other molecules in the mixture and allows it to be isolated.

Chromatography may be preparative or analytical. Preparative chromatography seeks to separate the components of a mixture for further use (and is thus a form of purification). Analytical chromatography normally operates with smaller amounts of material and seeks to measure the relative proportions of analytes in a mixture. The two are not mutually exclusive.

History

The history of chromatography spans from the mid-19th century to the 21st. Chromatography, literally "colour writing", was used—and named— in the first decade of the 20th century, primarily for the separation of plant pigments such as chlorophyll. New forms of chromatography developed in the 1930s and 1940s made the technique useful for a wide range of separation processes.

Some related techniques were developed in the 19th century (and even before), but the first true chromatography is usually attributed to Russian botanist Mikhail Semyonovich Tsvet, who used columns of calcium carbonate for separating plant pigments in the first decade of the 20th century during his research on chlorophyll.

Chromatography began to take its modern form following the work of Archer John Porter Martin and Richard Laurence Millington Synge in the 1940s and 1950s. They laid out the principles and basic techniques of partition chromatography, and their work spurred the rapid development of several lines of chromatography methods: paper chromatography, gas chromatography, and what would become known as high performance liquid chromatography. Since then, the technology has advanced rapidly. Researchers found that the principles underlying Tsvet's chromatography could be applied in many different ways, giving rise to the different varieties of chromatography described below. Simultaneously, advances continually improved the technical performance of chromatography, allowing the separation of increasingly similar molecules.

Chromatography Terms

- The *analyte* is the substance that is to be separated during chromatography.
- *Analytical chromatography* is used to determine the existence and possibly also the concentration of analyte(s) in a sample.
- A *bonded phase* is a stationary phase that is covalently bonded to the support particles or to the inside wall of the column tubing.

- A *chromatogram* is the visual output of the chromatograph. In the case of an optimal separation, different peaks or patterns on the chromatogram correspond to different components of the separated mixture.
- A *chromatograph* is equipment that enables a sophisticated separation e.g. gas chromatographic or liquid chroma-tographic separation.
- *Chromatography* is a physical method of separation in which the components to be separated are distributed between two phases, one of which is stationary (stationary phase) while the other (the mobile phase) moves in a definite direction.
- The *effluent* is the mobile phase leaving the column.
- An *immobilized phase* is a stationary phase which is immobilized on the support particles, or on the inner wall of the column tubing.
- The *mobile phase* is the phase which moves in a definite direction. It may be a liquid (LC and CEC), a gas (GC), or a supercritical fluid (supercritical-fluid chromatography, SFC). A better definition: The mobile phase consists of the sample being separated/analyzed and the solvent that moves the sample through the column. In one case of HPLC the solvent consists of a carbonate/bicarbonale solution and the sample is the anions being separated. The mobile phase moves through the chromatography column (the stationary phase) where the sample interacts with the stationary phase and is separated.
- *Preparative chromatography* is used to purify sufficient quantities of a substance for further use, rather than analysis.
- The *retention time* is the characteristic time it takes for a particular analyte to pass through the system (from the column inlet to the detector) under set conditions.

- The *sample* is the matter analysed in chromatography. It may consist of a single component or it may be a mixture of components. When the sample is treated in the course of an analysis, the phase or the phases containing the analytes of interest is/are referred to as the sample whereas everything out of interest separated from the sample before or in the course of the analysis is referred to as waste.
- The *solute* refers to the sample components in partition chromatography.
- The *solvent* refers to any substance capable of solubilizing other substance, and especially the liquid mobile phase in LC.
- The *stationary phase* is the substance which is fixed in place for the chromatography procedure. Examples include the silica layer in Chromatography Thin layer chromatography.

Techniques by Chromatographic Bed Shape

Column Chromatography

Column chromatography is a separation technique in which the stationary bed is within a tube. The particles of the solid stationary phase or the support coated with a liquid stationary phase may fill the whole inside volume of the tube (packed column) or be concentrated on or along the inside tube wall leaving an open, unrestricted path for the mobile phase in the middle part of the tube (open tubular column). Differences in rates of movement through the medium are calculated to different retention times of the sample.

In 1978, W. C. Still introduced a modified version of column chromatography called *flash column chromatography* (flash). The technique is very similar to the traditional column chromatography, except for that the solvent is driven through the column by applying positive pressure. This allowed most separations to be performed in less than 20 minutes, with improved separations compared to the old method. Modern flash chromatography systems are sold as pre-packed plastic cartridges, and the solvent is pumped through the cartridge. Systems may also be linked with detectors and fraction collectors providing automation. The introduction of gradient pumps resulted in quicker separations and less solvent usage.

A spreadsheet that assists in the successful development of flash columns has been developed. The spreadsheet estimates the retention volume and band volume of analytes, the fraction numbers expected to contain each analyte, and the resolution between adjacent peaks. This information allows users to select optimal parameters for preparative-scale separations before the flash column itself is attempted.

In expanded bed adsorption, a fluidized bed is used, rather than a solid phase made by a packed bed. This allows omission of initial clearing steps such as centrifugation and filtration, for culture broths or slurries of broken cells.

Planar Chromatography

Planar chromatography is a separation technique in which the stationary phase is present as or on a plane. The plane can be a paper, serving as such or impregnated by a substance as the stationary bed (paper chromatography) or a layer of solid particles spread on a support such as a glass plate (thin layer chromatography). Different compounds in the sample mixture travel different distances according to how strongly they interact with the stationary phase as compared to the mobile phase. The specific Retardation factor (Rf) of each chemical can be used to aid in the identification of an unknown substance.

Paper Chromatography

Paper chromatography is a technique that involves placing a small dot or line of sample solution onto a strip of *chromatography paper*. The paper is placed in a jar containing a shallow layer of solvent and sealed. As the solvent rises through the paper, it meets the sample mixture which starts to travel up the paper with the solvent. This paper is made of cellulose, a polar substance, and the compounds within the mixture travel farther if they are non-polar. More polar substances bond with the cellulose paper more quickly, and therefore do not travel as far.

Thin Layer Chromatography

Thin layer chromatography (TLC) is a widely-employed laboratory technique and is similar to paper chromatography. However, instead of using a stationary phase of paper, it involves a stationary phase of a thin layer of adsorbent like silica gel, alumina, or cellulose on a flat, inert substrate. Compared to paper, it has the advantage of faster runs, better separations, and the choice between different adsorbents. For even better resolution and to allow for quantitation, high-performance TLC can be used.

Displacement Chromatography

The basic principle of displacement chromatography is: A molecule with a high affinity for the chromatography matrix (the displacer) will compete effectively for binding sites, and thus displace all molecules with lesser affinities. There are distinct differences between displacement and elution chromatography. In elution mode, substances typically emerge from a column in narrow, Gaussian peaks. Wide separation of peaks, preferably to baseline, is desired in order to achieve maximum purification. The speed at which any component of a mixture travels down the column in elution mode depends on many factors. But for two substances to travel at different speeds, and thereby be resolved, there must be substantial differences in some interaction between the biomolecules and the chromatography matrix. Operating parameters are adjusted to maximize the effect of this difference. In many cases, baseline separation of the peaks can be achieved only with gradient elution and low column loadings. Thus, two drawbacks to elution mode chromatography, especially at the preparative scale, are operational complexity, due to gradient solvent pumping, and low throughput, due to low column loadings. Displacement chromatography has advantages over elution chromatography in that components are resolved into consecutive zones of pure substances rather than "peaks". Because the process takes advantage of the nonlinearity of the isotherms, a larger column feed can be separated on a given column with the purified components recovered at significantly higher concentrations.

Techniques by Physical State of Mobile Phase

Gas Chromatography

Gas Chromatography (GC), also sometimes known as Gas-Liquid Chromatography, (GLC), is a separation technique in which the mobile phase is a gas. Gas chromatography is always carried out in a column, which is typically "packed" or "capillary".

Gas Chromatography (GC) is based on a partition equilibrium of analyte between a solid stationary phase (often a liquid silicone-based material) and a mobile gas (most often Helium). The stationary phase is adhered to the inside of a small-diameter glass tube (a capillary column) or a solid matrix inside a larger metal tube (a packed column). It is widely used in analytical chemistry; though the high temperatures used in GC make it unsuitable for high molecular weight biopolymers or proteins (heat will denature them), frequently encountered in biochemistry, it is well suited for use in the petrochemical, environmental monitoring, and industrial chemical fields. It is also used extensively in chemistry research.

Liquid Chromatography

Liquid chromatography (LC) is a separation technique in which the mobile phase is a liquid. Liquid chromatography can be carried out either in a column or a plane. Present day liquid chromatography that generally utilizes very small packing particles and a relatively high pressure is referred to as high performance liquid chromatography (HPLC).

In the HPLC technique, the sample is forced through a column that is packed with irregularly or spherically shaped particles or a porous monolithic layer (stationary phase) by a liquid (mobile phase) at high pressure. HPLC is historically divided into two different sub-classes based on the polarity of the mobile and stationary phases. Technique in which the stationary phase is more polar than the mobile phase (e.g. toluene as the mobile phase, silica as the stationary phase) is called normal phase liquid chromatography (NPLC) and the opposite (e.g. water-methanol mixture as the mobile phase and C18 = octadecylsilyl as the stationary phase) is called reversed phase liquid chromatography (RPLC). Ironically the "normal phase" has fewer applications and RPLC is therefore used considerably more.

Specific techniques which come under this broad heading are listed below. It should also be noted that the following techniques can also be considered fast protein liquid chromatography if no pressure is used to drive the mobile phase through the stationary phase.

Affinity Chromatography

Affinity chromatography is based on selective non-covalent interaction between an analyte and specific molecules. It is very specific, but not very robust. It is often used in biochemistry in the purification of proteins bound to tags. These fusion proteins are labelled with compounds such as His-tags, biotin or antigens, which bind to the stationary phase specifically. After purification, some of these tags are usually removed and the pure protein is obtained.

Supercritical Fluid Chromatography

Supercritical fluid chromatography is a separation technique in which the mobile phase is a fluid above and relatively close to its critical temperature and pressure.

Techniques by Separation Mechanism

Ion Exchange Chromatography

Ion exchange chromatography uses ion exchange mechanism to separate analytes. It is usually performed in columns but can also be useful in planar mode. Ion exchange chromatography uses a charged stationary phase to separate charged compounds including amino acids, peptides, and proteins. In conventional methods the stationary phase is an ion exchange resin that carries charged functional groups which interact with oppositely charged groups of the compound to be retained. Ion exchange chromatography is commonly used to purify proteins using FPLC.

Size Exclusion Chromatography

Size exclusion chromatography (SEC) is also known as gel permeation chromatography (GPC) or gel filtration chromatography and separates molecules according to their size (or more accurately according to their hydrodynamic diameter or hydrodynamic volume). Smaller molecules are able to enter the pores of the media and, therefore, take longer to elute, whereas larger molecules are excluded from the pores and elute faster. It is generally a low resolution chromatography technique and thus it is often reserved for the final, "polishing" step of a purification. It is also useful for determining the tertiary structure and quaternary structure of purified proteins, especially since it can be carried out under native solution conditions.

Special Techniques

Reversed-phase Chromatography

Reversed-phase chromatography is an elution procedure used in liquid chromatography in which the mobile phase is significantly more polar than the stationary phase.

Two-dimensional Chromatography

In some cases, the chemistry within a given column can be insufficient to separate some analytes. It is possible to direct a series of unresolved peaks onto a second column with different physico-chemical (Chemical classification) properties. Since the mechanism of retention on this new solid support is different from the first dimensional separation, it can be possible to separate compounds that are indistinguishable by one-dimensional chromatography.

Fast Protein Liquid Chromatography (FPLC)

Fast protein liquid chromatography (FPLC) is a term applied to several chromatography techniques which are used to purify proteins. Many of these techniques are identical to those carried out under high performance liquid chromatography, however use of FPLC techniques are typically for preparing large scale batches of a purified product.

Countercurrent Chromatography

Countercurrent chromatography (CCC) is a type of liquid-liquid chromatography, where both the stationary and mobile phases are liquids. It involves mixing a solution of liquids, allowing them to settle into layers and then separating the layers.

Chiral Chromatography

Chiral chromatography involves the separation of stereoisomers. In the case of enantiomers, these have no chemical or physical differences apart from being three dimensional mirror images. Conventional chromatography or other separation processes are incapable of separating them. To enable chiral separations to take place, either the mobile phase or the stationary phase must themselves be made chiral, giving differing affinities between the analytes. Chiral chromatography HPLC columns (with a chiral stationary phase) in both normal and reversed phase are commercially available.

6

Gas Phase Chemistry Study during Deposition of a-Si: H and μc-Si: H Films by HWCVD using Quadrupole Mass Spectrometry

Abstract

Amorphous and microcrystalline silicon films were deposited by HWCVD under different deposition conditions and the gas phase chemistry was studied by in situ Quadrupole Mass Spectrometry. Attempt is made to correlate the properties of the films with the gas phase chemistry during deposition. Interestingly, unlike in PECVD, partial pressure of H_2 is higher than any other species during deposition of a-Si:H as well as μc-Si:H. Effect of hydrogen dilution on film properties and on concentration of various chemical species in the gas phase is studied. For low hydrogen dilution $[H_2]/[SiH_4]$ from 0 to 1 (where $[SiH_4]$ is 10 sccm), all films deposited are amorphous with photoconductivity gain of ~ 106. During deposition of these amorphous films SiH_2 was dominant in gas phase next to $[H_2]$. Interestingly $[Si]/[SiH_2]$ ratio increases from 0.4 to 0.5 as dilution increased from 0 to 1, and further to more than 1 for higher hydrogen dilution leading to [Si] dominance. At hydrogen dilution ratio 20, consequently films deposited were microcrystalline.

Deposition precursors involved in Hot Wire Chemical Vapor Deposition (HWCVD) are claimed to be different than those involved in Plasma enhanced chemical vapor deposition (PECVD).

Unlike PECVD where in, there is a possibility of a range of ions and radicals existing in the deposition ambient, only limited radicals have been identified in HWCVD Since radical precursors influence growth and the film properties strongly, monitoring their concentration is important from the point of view of correlating the gas phase chemistry with film properties. Till now different groups have tried to detect the different chemical species in HWCVD SiH_3 and Si_2H_6 were suggested to be the largest and also the film forming species. At filament temperatures > 1600°C, Si was shown as dominant whereas for polysilicon deposition conditions SiH_2 was shown as dominating Origin of SiH_2 or reactions leading to SiH_2 formation are still unclear. It has been reported that it may be due to heterogeneous pyrolysis of SiH_4 on hot surfaces other than the filament Though reactions leading to higher order silane i.e. Si_2H_x are favorable their proportion in gas phase is very small Whereas, few researchers claim the presence of significant Si_2H_x radicals in HWCVD. These results are contradictory to each other and create ambiguity regarding presence of higher order silanes in HWCVD.

In HWCVD, the chemical composition at the filament would be different from that away from the filament depending on the gas pressure. At low pressures, (less than ~0.1 mTorr), mean free path of radicals originating from the filament is of the order of substrate to filament distance.

Hence, precursors produced due to dissociation of gases on the filament will be dominant in the atmosphere. But at higher pressures (~30mTorr), mean free path is quite less leading to more frequent collisions of radicals present in the chamber. As a result more radical – radical reactions occur and we see different deposition chemistry at higher pressures. It has been seen that hydrogen dilution is one of the key parameters that controls the film properties urther it has been shown that the effect of hydrogen dilution observed in PECVD is not same as observed in HWCVD Thus, study of gas phase precursors in HWCVD for various hydrogen dilutions is important. In this work, we show that gas phase chemical composition varies significantly with hydrogen dilution in HWCVD leading to different physical properties of the films.

Experimental

Films were deposited with hydrogen dilution (H_2/SiH_4 flow rate ratio). Other parameters like the substrate temperature (TS) = 250°C, filament temperature (T_F) = 1800°C, total pressure (P) = 30 mTorr- were kept constant. Characterization for chemical bonding of the films was done by FTIR spectroscopy and structural characterization by Atomic Force Microscopy. Optoelectronic properties of the films such as bandgap, dark ($\sigma\alpha$) and photo (σph) conductivity were determined. Gas phase analysis was carried out with the help of Quadrupole Mass Spectrometer.

Results

Deposition in the Low H_2 Dilution Regime

Hydrogen dilution $[H_2]/[SiH_4]$ for these films was varied from 0 to 1 (SiH_4 flow =10 sccm and H_2 flow was varied from 0 to 10 sccm). All the films deposited with this dilution were amorphous as can be seen by dark conductivity (~ 10^{-10} (ohm.cm)$^{-1}$) and photo conductivity gain ~ 10^6.

Deposition rate RD, dark and photoconductivity of these a-Si:H films for increasing hydrogen H_2 = 10 sccm. An increase in σph of almost 1 order was observed as the H_2 flow was increased from 0 to 6, which then remains constant. The σd however shows very little increase throughout. As a result the photo-conductivity gain variation $\sigma ph/\sigma d$ shows a maximum and saturation above 6 sccm of H_2 flow. FTIR transmission spectra of these show a signature at 2000 cm^{-1} corresponding to Si-H stretching. The symmetry in the 2000 cm^{-1} peak reflects the negligible contribution from Si-H_2 bonding. The microstructure factor R where $R = I_{2100}/(I_{2100} + I_{2000})$, which is a measure of the film quality, improves from 0.21 to 0.06 as hydrogen dilution increases from 0 to 0.6.

Deposition in the High H_2 Dilution Regime

Another set of films was deposited with high H_2 dilution i. e. at 20 (SiH_4 = 1sccm and H_2 = 20 sccm). The films were micro-crystalline in nature.

However the AFM studies of different samples indicate a variation in grain size from 100nm to 320nm with increasing substrate temperature. Figure 6.1 shows a typical AFM image of microcrystalline silicon sample indicating a grain size ~ 300nm.

Gas Phase Composition Analysis

Quadrupole mass analysis results, during deposition of the films with low H_2 dilution are shown in fig. 6.3. Mass spectra for Hot Wire ON are shown by solid line (—) and those obtained during hot wire off are shown by dotted line (……). Contribution due to cracking of gases in ionizer of QMS is taken care by normalization of signals individually.

Important observations after turning the Hot Wire ON are as follows:

1. First striking observation is that the [H_2] partial pressure in the chamber increases by more than an order, unlike that observed in PECVD.

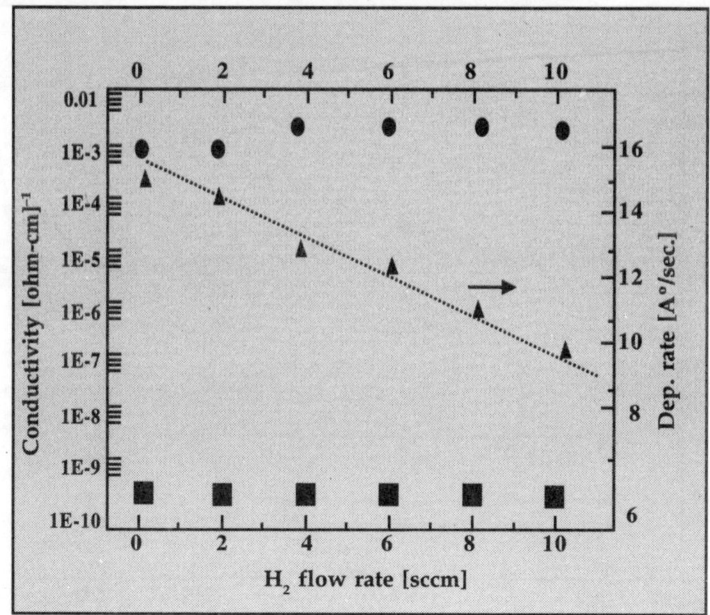

0 2 4 6 8 10
0.01
1E-3
1E-4
1E-5
1E-6
1E-7
1E-8
1E-9
1E-10
Conductivity [ohm-cm]-1
16
14
12
10
8
6
Dep. rate [A°/sec.]
0 2 4 6 8 10
H2 flow rate [sccm]

Fig. 6.1

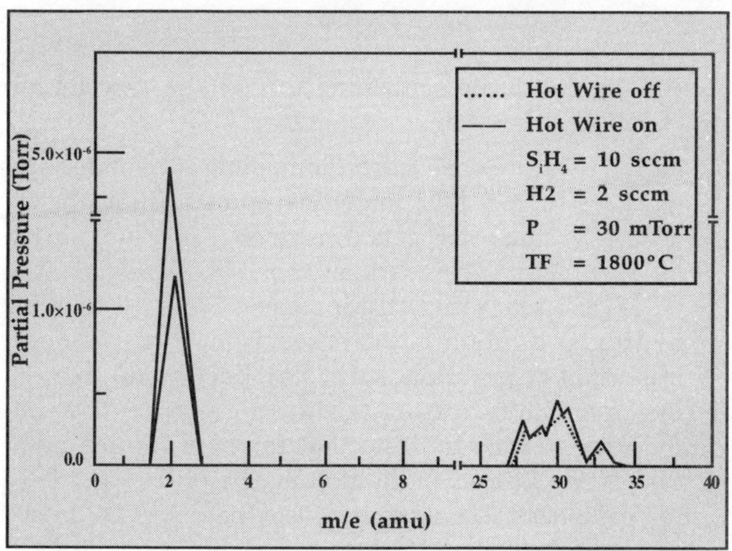

...... Hot Wire off
—— Hot Wire on
SiH4 = 10 sccm
H2 = 2 sccm
P = 30 mTorr
TF = 1800°C
5.0×10-6
1.0×10-6
0.0
Partial Pressure (Torr)
0 2 4 6 8 25 30 35 40
m/e (amu)

Fig. 6.2

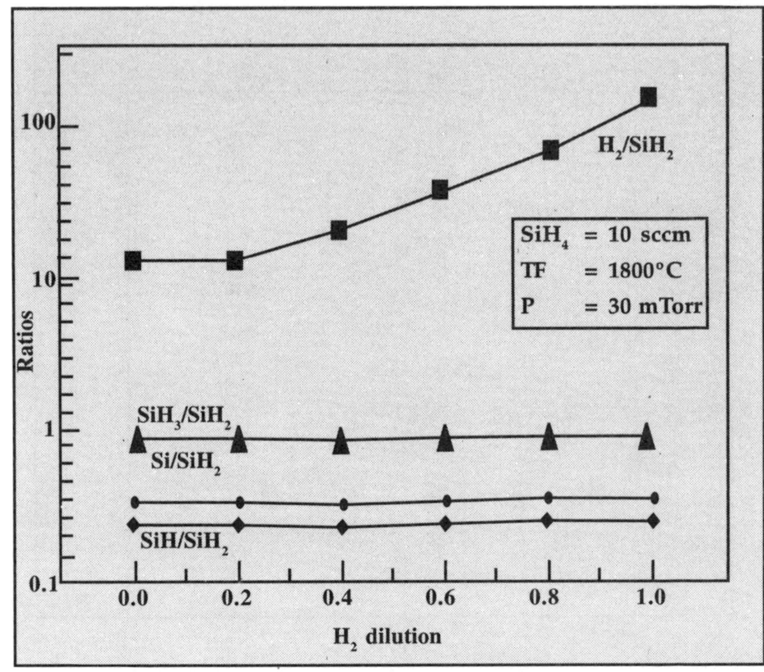

Fig. 6.3

2. Among the silicon containing species, the concentration of [SiH_2] is highest.

3. Partial pressure of all silicon containing species decreases whereas that of [H_2] increases upon turning the Hot Wire ON, since SiH_4 gets consumed. l pressure i.e. [X]/[SiH_2], where X stands for any species. As seen the ratio [H_2]/[SiH_2] significantly increases from 10 to 110 as hydrogen dilution is increased from 0 to 1. Another important observation is that [Si]/[SiH_2] ratio shows an increase with increasing H_2 dilution. The trends seen in these two ratios indicate that for H_2 dilutions higher than 1 would lead to the dominance of [H_2] and [S_i] in the gas phase. The issue here is, what effect could such an abundance of [H_2] and [Si] have on the film

properties? For this we looked at the films deposited in the low $[H_2]$ dilution regime as well as those deposited in the high $[H_2]$ dilution regime by X-ray diffraction and atomic force microscopy (AFM). What we see is extremely interesting. The films deposited at high $[H_2]$ dilution turn out to be micro-crystalline, confirmed by AFM measurements.

Simultaneously we studied the gas phase chemistry for the $[H_2]$ dilution ranging from 0 to 1 (low H_2 dilution) and at higher dilution of 20. The results of these are shown in Fig. 6.4. This figure once again depicts the variation of the ratio $[X]/[SiH_2]$ as the $[H_2]$ dilution is increased from 0 to 1 and then to 20. One observes an increase of more than two orders of magnitude in $[H_2]/[SiH_2]$ ratio while the $[Si]/[SiH_2]$ ratio increases by 7 times as the $[H_2]$ dilution increases to 20.

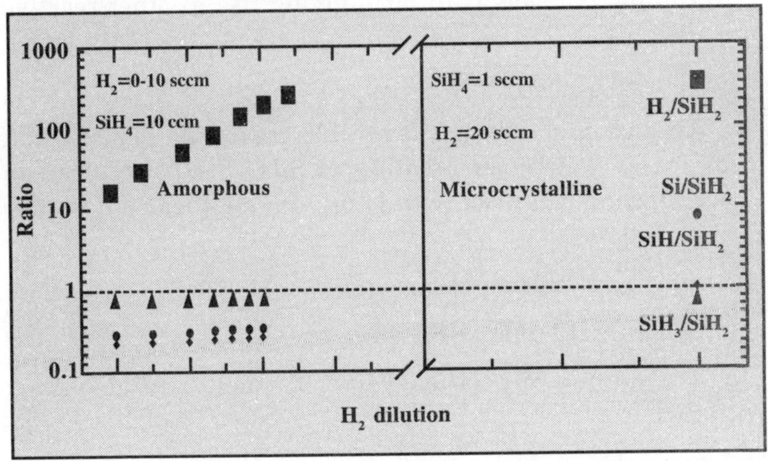

Fig. 6.4

As can be seen from the results, SiH_2 is the dominant radical during the deposition of a-Si:H material, while Si is dominant during deposition of micro-crystalline silicon where a high hydrogen dilution is employed. Reaction paths leading to the dominance of these species are explained below.

Low Hydrogen Dilution

Basic reaction for the dissociation of SiH_4 on the tungsten filament surface is:

SiH_4•¨ $Si + 4H$ (6.1)

Desorption of the separated Si and H atoms from the filament surface depends on filament temperature At higher filament temperatures separation of dissociated Si and H from filament is effective. At filament temperature of 1800°C, dissociated Si is less likely to permeate in tungsten filament to form tungsten silicide and gets desorbed readily from filament surface . These desorbed Si and H atoms undergo gas phase reactions with source gases SiH_4 and H_2 to produce different radicals. Various reaction pathways have been suggested.

Atomic H reacts with SiH4 giving rise to other reactive species,

$H + SiH_4$•¨ $SiH_3 + H_2$ (6.2)

Though SiH_3 is most favorable radical as per reaction (6.2), it is a source for creation of SiH_2. SiH_3 produced in above reaction can react with H or with another SiH_3 to give SiH_2 as follows.

$SiH_3 + H$•¨ $SiH_2 + H_2$ (6.3)

$SiH_3 + SiH_3$•¨ $SiH_2 + SiH_4$ (6.4)

The atomic Si produced over filament can also react with SiH_4.

$Si + SiH_4$•¨ Si_2H_4

* •¨ 2SiH2 (6.5)

•¨ $SiH + SiH_3$ (6.6)

•¨ $Si_2H_2 + H_2$ (6.7)

•¨ Si_2H_4 (6.8)

The insignificant contribution of Si_2H_2 and Si_2H_4 to the observed mass spectra confirm the argument of Holt et. al. that the reaction (6.7) and (6.8) have very less probability.

Thus SiH_2, SiH_3, SiH and Si are the main gas species in the ambient. Though SiH_3 is more favorable species produced by reaction (6.2), it is not seen as dominant in gas phase since it is major source of SiH_2 through reactions 3 and 4. Thus, SiH_2 is the most favorable species as it is the product of most of the gas phase reactions (6.3), (6.4) and (6.5).This also has been observed in mass spectrometric analysis as SiH_2 dominance during a-Si:H deposition. It will be too early to come to a conclusion that SiH_2 is the film forming species. If that is the case, it can obey Scott's model of formation of a-Si:H films.

In case of high hydrogen dilution, SiH_4 fraction in gas phase will be low. After primary reaction of dissociation of silane as atomic Si and H, there is less SiH_4 available to react with Si and H than in the former case. Hence SiH_3 produced by way of reaction (6.2) will be low. Consequently, there will be less SiH_2, since SiH_3 is the source of SiH_2 through reactions (6.3) and (6.4). Thus less availability of silane reduces the partial pressures of SiH_3 and SiH_2 in the gas phase. This results in less consumption of atomic Si, produced at the filament, through reactions (6.5) ,(6.6), (6.7) and (6.8). Most of the atomic Si manages to reach the substrate leading to its dominance in the gas phase.

Whether the predominance of atomic Si helps in the growth of μc-Si:H is a matter of concern. Though sticking coefficient of Si is higher, due to high hydrogen coverage of substrate surface Si has enough surface mobility and this gives more ordered structure. Effect of higher sticking coefficient of Si is overshadowed due to atomic hydrogen etching since it etches away the disordered structures. We think that the composite effect involving a highly disordered network getting converted to the μc-phase through hydrogen etching may be responsible for the observed μc-phase in these films. This is not the first time that an attempt is made to understand the growth mechanism of μc Si:H films. There have been various models that have been proposed. However, there has been no study up till now where direct evidence of different gas chemistry has been shown to exist during the deposition of amorphous and microcrystalline material. We, no doubt believe in the important role that surface reactions play in structural evolution during thin film growth. But the strong evidence that has been gathered during the present study, clearly emphasize the role that different species present in the gas phase could play in evolving the structure of the growing film. This is particularly true for low-pressure processes like the HWCVD. The present study also reveals that life times of the species are significantly long to affect the growth characteristics.

Secondly, the role of H_2 in promoting microcrystalline growth is once again clearly brought out by the present study. One of the observations i.e., a higher [Si]/[SiH_2] ratio during microcrystalline film growth implies that atomic Silicon also plays a role in the formation of the microcrystalline phase.

Conclusion

Gas phase species produced during the dissociation of SiH_4 + H_2 gas mixture have been analyzed by QMS. These results clearly indicate the significance of different chemical species in evolving the structural aspects of the deposited films. During low hydrogen dilution, SiH_2 is dominant leading to a-Si:H films whereas, Si is dominant for high hydrogen dilution giving microcrystalline films. Determination of the exact mechanism through which these species affect the growth kinetics and the subsequent structure of the films is of course a matter of further research.

7

Gas Phase Chemistry of Citronellol with Ozone and OH Radical

Rate Constants and Products

In the USA, it is estimated that over 30 million of the total 89 million workers in indoor environments are affected by the work environment in the form of eye, nose and throat irritations, headache, and fatigue. These health complaints have an estimated impact on worker productivity of tens of billions of dollars annually. Unfortunately there is currently no direct correlation between these complaints and a specific pollutant In fact, exposures to multiple pollutants in the indoor environment may be responsible. There is growing interest in understanding the role volatile organic compound (VOC) gas-phase reaction products have on human health.

The indoor environment chemistry by Weschler highlights several research areas important to the field. Significant observations from this review paper are that there are still several fundamental questions regarding the gas-phase chemistry of indoor environments, and that the indoor environment is chemically more complex than previously thought. Experimental evidence has demonstrated that several initiator species such as ozone (O_3), hydroxyl radical (OH) and nitrate radical (NO_3) are likely to be resent in indoor air and the VOC concentrations indoors are higher by a factor of ten or more than typically found in outdoor environments.

Oxygenated organic compounds, such as ethers, alcohols and esters, are becoming more prevalent in the indoor environment as they are substituted for other chemicals in consumer products. One such compound of interest is 3,7-dimethyl-6-octen-1-ol a volatile organic alcohol that is a significant component of bug/insect repellants and hard-surface cleaners. While several hydroxyl radical (OH)+oxygenated organic and ozone (O_3)+oxygenated organic bimolecular rate constants are well known, a few recent studies of the products from OH+oxygenated organic reactions have illustrated the complexity of their gas-phase reaction mechanisms.

In the work presented here, the rate constant of the OH radical with citronellol was measured by the relative rate method. Additionally, the citronellol/O_3 rate constant was also determined by monitoring the decrease in the ozone concentration in an excess of citronellol. The products of the OH+citronellol and O_3 + citronellol reactions are also reported. Neither the OH rate constant, O_3 rate constant nor the respective reaction products for citronellol have been reported previously.

Apparatus and Materials

Sampling for the citronellol/OH kinetics experiments was performed using a polydimethylsolixane/ divinylbenzene solid phase micro-extraction (SPME) fiber (Supelco, Milwaukee, WI, 57310-U) assembly which was inserted into a 6.4mm Swagelok (Solon, OH) fitting attached to a 60–90 L Teflons R-film chamber. The SPME fiber was exposed for 5 min within the chamber, and then inserted into the injector of a Hewlett Packard (HP) 5890 gas chromatograph with a 5972 mass selective detector (GC/MS) and HP software. The GC temperature program used was: injection port was set to 250 °C, and oven temperature began at 40 °C for 6 min and was ramped 10 °Cmin^{-1} to 260 °C and held for 3 min. Experiments to measure the reaction of ozone with 3, 7-dimethyl-6-octen-1-ol were conducted using a similar chamber as described above, except the ozone concentration was monitored using a UV photometric ozone analyzer (Thermo Environmental model 49-C Franklin, MA).

Identification of reaction products was made using *O*-(2, 3, 4, 5, 6-pentafluorobenzyl) hydroxylamine (PFBHA) to derivatize carbonyl products, while xylic acid products were derivatized using PFBHA and BSTFA. Experimental methods for reaction product identification were similar to methods used for kinetic experiments, except the reference compound was excluded from the reaction mixture.

Derivatized reaction products were analyzed using a Varian (Palo Alto, CA) 3800/Saturn 2000 he electron impact (EI) and chemical ionization (CI) modes. Compound separation was achieved by a J&W Scientific (Folsom, CA) DB-5MS (0.32mmi.d., 30-m long, 1 μm film thickness) column and the following GC oven parameters: 60 °C for 1 min then 10 °Cmin^{-1} to 280 °C and held for 10 min. Samples were injected in the splitless mode, and the GC injector was returned to split mode 1min after sample injection, with the following injector temperature parameters: 60 °C for 1 min then 180 °Cmin^{-1} to 250 °C and held to the end of the chromatographic run. The Saturn 2000 ion trap mass amine (FC-43). Full-scan EI ionization spectra were collected from m/z 40–650. Acetonitrile was the chemical ionization reagent used for all CI spectra. When possible, commercially available samples of the identified products were derivatized and subsequently analyzed to verify matching ion spectra and chromatographic retention times.

Hydroxyl radicals, which are among the primary oxidizing radicals in the indoor environment, were generated from the photolysis of methyl nitrite (CH_3ONO) in the presence of nitric oxide (NO) in air. CH_3ONO was prepared in gram quantities and stored in a lecture bottle at room temperature. The CH_3ONO purity (>95%) was verified by GC/MS. Ozone was produced by photolyzing air with a mercury pen lamp in a separate Teflon chamber. Aliquots of this O_3/air mixture were added to the Teflon reaction chamber using a gas-tight syringe.

All compounds were used as received and had the following purities: from Sigma-Aldrich (Milwaukee, WI): cyclohexane (99.9%), hexane (99%), limonene (99%), 3,7-dimethyl-6-octen-1-ol (citronellol) (99%), 3-carene (90%), acetonitrile (99.93%), *N,O*-bis (trimethylsilyl) trifluoroacetamide (BSTFA) (99+%), *O*-(2, 3, 4, 5, 6-pentafluorobenzyl)- hydroxylamine hydrochloride (PFBHA) (98+%); from Fisher Scientific (Fairlawn, NJ): methanol (99%); from Spectrum Analytical (New Brunswick, NJ): methylene chloride (99.5%). Nitric oxide (99+% pure) was obtained as a 4942 ppm mixture in nitrogen from Butler Gases (Morrisville, PA). Helium (UHP grade), the carrier gas, was supplied by Amerigas (Sabraton, WV) and used as received. Experiments were carried out at (297±3)K and 1 atmosphere pressure.

Experimental Procedures

The experimental procedures for determining the citronellol+OH reaction kinetics were similar to those described previously.

The rate equations for reactions (7.1) and (7.2) are combined and integrated, resulting in the following equation:

$$\text{Citronellol} + \text{OH} \xrightarrow{k_{\text{OH+Citronellol}}} \text{Products} \qquad (7.1)$$

$$\text{Reference} + \text{OH} \xrightarrow{k_{\text{Ref}}} \text{Products} \qquad (7.2)$$

The rate equations for reactions (7.1) and (7.2) are combined and integrated, resulting in the following equation:

$$\ln\left(\frac{[\text{Citronellol}]_0}{[\text{Citronellol}]_t}\right) = \frac{k_{\text{OH+Citronellol}}}{k_{\text{Ref}}}\ln\left(\frac{[\text{Ref}]_0}{[\text{Ref}]_t}\right)$$

If reaction with OH is the only removal mechanism for citronellol and reference, a plot of ln ($[\text{Citronellol}]_0$/ $[\text{Citronellol}]_t$) versus ln($[\text{Ref}]_0/[\text{Ref}]_t$) yields a straight line with an intercept of zero. Multiplying the slope of this linear plot by k_{Ref} yields $k_{OH+citronellol}$. The OH rate constant experiments for citronellol employed the use of two reference compounds: limonene and 3-carene. The use of two different reference compounds with different OH rate constants more definitively assured the accuracy of the citronellol/OH rate constant and demonstrates that other reactions are not removing citronellol.

For the citronellol/OH kinetic experiments the typical concentrations of the pertinent species in the 60-90L Teflon chamber were 0.3-0.7ppm ($0.7\text{-}1.7\times10^{13}$ moleculecm^{-3}) citronellol, 0.3–0.6ppm ($0.7\text{–}1.5\times10^{13}$ moleculecm^{-3}) reference, 10 ppm (231013 moleculecm^{-3}) CH_3ONO, and 0–0.6ppm (0–1.4 10^{13} moleculecm^{-3}) NO in air. Citronellol was diluted in a 30:70 (v:v) solution with methanol. Methanol was chosen because the methanol/OH reaction did not yield chromatographically interfering products. Furthermore, for the methanol/O_3 reaction, methanol does not react with O_3 because of the absence of a double bond. The gas-phase mixtures were allowed to reach equilibrium before initial species concentration ($[X]_0$) samples were collected. Typically, four photolysis intervals of 10-20 s each were used on the reaction mixture for a combined total photolysis time of approximately 40-60 s. The total ion chromatogram (TIC) from the HP 5972 mass selective detector was used to determine itronellol and reference concentrations.

The experimental procedures for the determination of the citronellol+O_3 reaction kinetics were similar to those described previously.

$$\text{Citronellol} + O_3 \xrightarrow{kO_{3+\text{Citronellol}}} \text{Products} \quad (7.3)$$

Approximately 0.1ppm (2.46×10^{12} moleculecm^{-3}) of ozone was injected into the reaction chamber as it was being filled with air and citronellol. The range of initial citronellol concentrations was 0.2-0.6 ppm ($0.4\text{-}1.5 \times 10^{13}$ moleculecm^{-3}).

The chamber was connected within 5 s to the Thermo Electron UV photometric ozone analyzer Model 49C and ozone concentration measurements integrated over 10 s time intervals were collected up to a total of 420 s. Cyclohexane (410 ppm, 4.11018 molecules cm^{-3}) was added to the citronellol/O_3 reaction product experiments to scavenge OH radicals.

Derivatization of the carbonyl reaction products was initiated by flowing of 15–25 L of chamber contents at 3.8 L min^{-1} through 3mL of acetonitrile in an impinger with no effort to prevent acetonitrile evaporation during sample collection. The sample was removed from the impinger and 200 mL of 0.02M PFBHA was added to derivatize the carbonyl reaction products to oximes over a 24–48 h time period in the dark. The reacted solutions were gently blown to dryness with UHP N^2, reconstituted with 100 μL of methanol and 1 mL of the reconstituted solution was injected onto the Varian 3800/Saturn 2000 GC/MS system.

The derivatization of hydroxy groups (either alcohol or carboxylic acid) was achieved by subsequent addition of 20 mL of commercially available BSTFA to the PFBHA oximes reconstituted with 100 mL of hexane:methylene chloride (1:1). These PFBHA/BSTFA solutions were heated to approximately hen 1 μL of the solution was injected into the Varian 3800/ Saturn 2000 GC/MS system.

To determine possible chromatographic interferences from reference/OH reaction products, both citronellol and the reference compounds were reacted with the OH radical in separate experiments and analyzed as described previously. No chromatographic interferences were observed. All measurements were at least duplicated. A relative standard deviation (the data set standard deviation divided by the data set average) of approximately 3.4% was achieved with the described sampling methods utilizing the HP 5890/5972 GC/MS system.

Citronellol/OH Reaction Rate Constant

The ln ($[Ref]_0/[Ref]_t$ term is divided by the respective reference rate constant (limonene (164±41) × 10^{-12} cm^3 $molecule^{-1}$ s^{-1} and 3-carene (88±22) × 10^{-12} cm^3 $molecule^{-1}$ s^{-1} (Atkinson, 1989, 1994, 2003; Bardley et. al., 2001) and multiplied by 10^{-12} cm^3 $molecule^{-1}$ s^{-1}, resulting in a unitless number. The yields a slope that is equal to the OH/citronellol rate constant, $k_{OH + citronellol}$, *divided by* 10^{-12} cm^3 $molecule^{-1}$ s^{-1}. This modification allows for a direct comparison of the two reference compound/citronellol data sets. The data points at the origin are experimental points because pre-irradiation, $t = 0$, data showed no detectable loss of citronellol or reference. The error in the rate constant stated above is the 95% confidence level from the random uncertainty in the slope. Incorporating the uncertainties associated with the reference rate constants (±25% for limonene and 3-carene) used to derive the citronellol/OH rate constant yields a final value for $k_{OH+citronellol}$, of (170±43) × 10^{-12} cm^3 $molecule^{-1}$ s^{-1} (Atkinson, 1989, 1994, 2003). The citronellol/OH rate constant, $k_{OH + citronellol}$, has not been previously reported. The observed rate constant is comparable to a $k(calc)_{OH + citronellol}$ = 98 × 10^{-12} cm^3 $molecule^{-1}$ s^{-1}, calculated using the Environmental Protection Agency's rate constant calculation software. AOP-WIN v1.91 (US Environmental Protection Agency, 2000).

Citronellol/O_3 Reaction Rate Constant

The experimental conditions, described above, to determine the citronellol/O_3 reaction rate constant resulted in a first order decrease in ozone concentration in excess citronellol over a 7 min monitoring period. Analysis of the data, shown in Fig. 7.1 resulted in the determination of the citronellol/O_3 rate constant of (2.4±0.1) × 10^{-16} cm^3 $molecule^{-1}$ s^{-1}. The error in this rate constant is the 95% confidence interval from the random uncertainty in the slope. The estimated rate constant can be compared with a $k(calc)_{O3 + citronellol}$ = 4.3 × 10^{-16} cm^3 $molecule^{-1}$ s^{-1}, calculated using the Environmental Protection Agency's rate constant calculation software. AOP-WIN v1.91) (US Environmental Protection Agency, 2000).

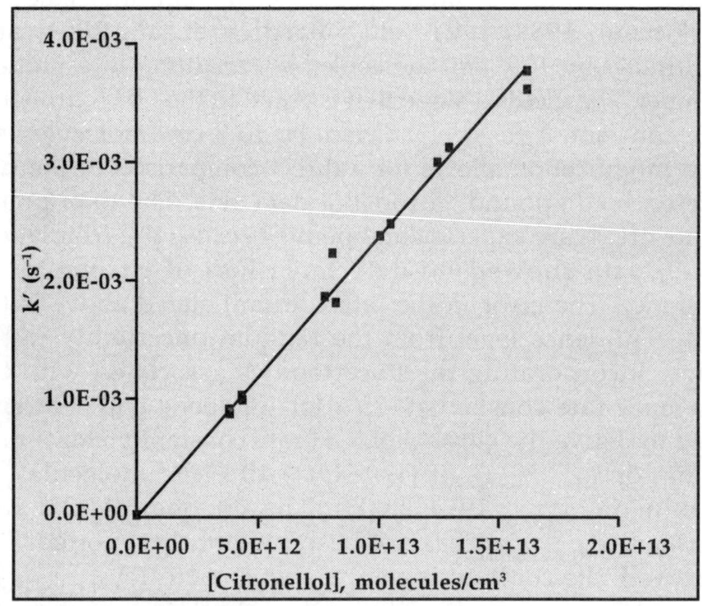

Fig. 7.1: **First order loss rate of ozone versus citronellol concentration. The slope yields a citronellol + ozone reaction rate constant of (2.4±0.1) × 10^{-16} cm^3 $molecules^{-1}$ s^{-1}**

Citronellol/OH and Citronellol/O3 Reaction Products

The reaction products observed from the initial citronellol/OH hydrogen abstraction or OH addition or O_3 addition to the carbon-carbon double bond are listed in Table 7.1. The citronellol/OH and citronellol/O_3 reaction products observed and positively identified using the pure compound for verification by derivatization were: acetone, ethanedial (glyoxal, HC(=O)C(=O)H), 2-oxopropanal (methylglyoxal, $CH_3C(=O)C(=O)H$). Structures and ions used to identify these compounes are listed in Table 7.1. Elucidation of the other major reaction product, 6-hydroxy-4-methylhexanal, was facilitated by mass spectrometry of the derivatized reaction product coupled with plausible citronellol/OH and citronellol/O_3 reaction mechanisms based on previously published volatile organic compound/OH and volatile organic compound/O_3 gas-phase reaction as described below (Atkinson, 1989; Bradley et. al., 2001; Smith et al., 1992, 1995; Veillerot et al., 1996; Wallington et al., 1993; Wells, 2004; Wells et al., 1996; Wyatt et al., 1999).

Derivatization of nonsymmetric carbonyls using PFBHA or PFBHA/BSTFA typically resulted in multiple chromatographic peaks due to geometric isomers of the oximens. Identification of multiple peaks of the same oxime compound is relatively simple since the mass spectra for each chromatographic peak of a particular oxime are almost identical. Typically, the PFBHA-derivatized oximes' (generic structure: $F_5C_6CH_2ON=C(R_1)(R_2)$) mes' spectra included an ion at *m/z* 181 ($[CH_2C_6F_5]^+$ fragment) with a large relative intensity (>40%) and a $[\text{PFBHA oxime} + 181]^+$ ion (due to reactions in the ion trap mass spectrometer) (Yu et al., 1998). In most cases, the *m/z* 181 ion relatively intensity for the chromatographic peaks due to citronellol/OH and citronellol/O_3 reaction product oximes was either the largest or one of the largest in the mass spectrum and was used to generate selected ion chromatograms (Yu et al., 1998). The mass spectra of compounds that were additionally

Table 7.1: Molecular structure of citronellol/OH and citronellol/O_3 reaction products

Retention time (min)	Name	Molecular weight (amu)	Structure	CI ions observed	EI ions observed (relative intensity
11.3	Acetone	58	 O	254	181(100),253(14)
19.67	6-Hydroxy-4-methylhexanal	130	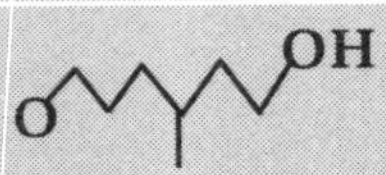 O OH	326	181(100), 252(75), 325(40)
21.0 21.2	Ethanedial	58	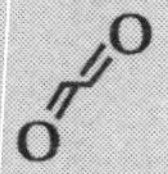 O O	449	181(100), 448(33)
21.1	2-Oxopropanal	72	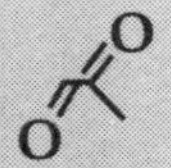 O O	463	181(100), 265(16), 462(11)

derivatized with BSTFA contained *m/z* 73 ions from the $[Si(CH_3)_3]^+$ fragments (Yu et al., 1998). The product data are described below.

The following chronological chromatographic retention time results and mass spectra data were observed utilizing PFBHA or PFBHA/BSTFA derivatization and the Varian 3800/Saturn 2000 GC/MS system. The reaction products reported here had chromatographic peak areas proportional to initial citronellol concentration and were observal only after OH initiation of citronellol/methanol/methyl nitrite/NO/air mixtures or addition of O_3 to citronellol/methanol/air. Derivatization experiments performed in the absence of citronellol, but in the presence of all other chemicals in the reaction chamber (methanon/methyl nitrite/NO/air) did not result in any of the data reported below except for small amounts (as noted by chromatographic peak areas) of acetone, 2-oxopropanal, and ethanedial.

Acetone was also observed in pre-photoinitiated citronellol/OH or pre-ozonated citronellol/O_3 derivatization samples. However, the acetone, 2-oxopropanol, and ethanedial oxime peak areas increased significantly, between 30% and 50%, with citronellol/OH or citronellol/O_3 reaction initiation, indicating that acetone, 2-oxopropanal and ethanedial are likely products of the citronellol + OH and citronellol + O_3 reactions.

Acetone

Acetone was identified as both a citronellol/OH and a citronellol/O3 reaction product using the Agilent 6890/5973 GC/MS system and PFBHA derivatization method described above. The acetone oxime (PFBHA = C $(CH_3)_2$) was observed at approximately 11.4 min employing the Varian 3800/Saturn 2000 GC/ion trap mass spectrometer system described above. Acetone oxime was synthesized to confirm this chromatographic assignment. Acetone oxime was observed in pre-photolysis samples, but the peak area increased upon reaction initiation.

Oxime at Retention time 19.7 min

The oxime observed with chromatographic peak at retention time of 19.7 min had ions of *m/z* (relative intensity) 84 (19%), 181 (100%), 252 (75%), and 325 (40%). Using acetonitrile for chemical ionization an *M* + 1 ion of *m/z* of 326 was observed. Using the derivatized molecular weight of 325 for the oxime suggests a carbonyl compound with a molecular weight of 130. The single chromatographic peak suggests an aldehyde structure or a symmetric ketone structure. A proposed citronellol/OH and citronellol/O_3 reaction product of 6-hydroxy-4-methylhexanal (Table 7.1) was made based upon the observed data. Further confirmation of the proposed identity of this product was made using chemical ionization and PFBHA/BSTRA derivatization. Mass spectra from CI analysis showed two peaks with *m/z* 398 ([*M* + 1]) at 20.1 and 20.2 min, which is the combination of the derivatized PFBHA oxime {*m/z* 325) with the BSTFA derivatized alcohol (*m/z* 72).

Ethanedial (Glyoxal, HC (=O)C (=O) H)

The chromatographic peaks for the oxime observed at 21.0 and 21.2 min was observed as a reaction product of citronellol/OH and citronellol/O3 had ions at *m/z* (relative intensity) 181 (100%) and 448 (33%). The *m/z* 448 ion is the result of a double PFBHA derivatization indicating a reaction product with a molecular weight of 58. Using acetonitrile for chemical ionization an *M* + 1 ion of *m/z* of 449 was observed for the PFBHA derivatized sample. The PFBHA-glyoxal oxime was synthesized to confirm this chromatographic assignment.

2-Oxopropanal (methylglyoxal, $CH_3C(=O)C(=O)H$)

The chromatographic peaks for the oxime observed at 21.1 and 21.4min was observed as a reaction product of citronellol/OH and citronellol/O_3 had ions at *m/s* (relative intensity) 181 (100%), 265 (16%), and 462 (11%). The *m/z* 462 ion is the result of a double PFBHA derivatization indicating a reaction product with a molecular weight of 72. Using acetonitrile for chemical ionization an $M + 1$ ion of m/z of 463 was observed for the PFBHA derivatized sample. The PFBHA-methylglyoxal oxime was synthesized to confirm this chromatographic assignment and the second chromatogrphic peak for PFBHA-methylglyoxal overlaps with the 21.0 min peak of PFBHA-glyoxal.

Discussion

OH reacts with citronellol by H-atom abstraction or OH addition to the carbon-carbon double bond (Atkinson, 1989; Atkinson and Aschmann, 1993). The "reactive structure" of citronellol can be drawn as shown in Structure 1. The sites labeled I, II and III identified in Structure 1 contribute approximately 88%, 3% and 4%, respectively, to the calculated citronellol/OH rate constant of 98×10^{-12} cm^3 $molecule^{-1}$ s^{-1} (US Environmental Protection Agency, 2000) which is slower than the measured valued reported here $(170 \pm 43) \times 10^{-12}$ cm^3 $molecule^{-1}$ s^{-1}.

Ozone reacts with citronellol by addition to the carbon—carbon double bond (site I, Structure 1). The calculated citronellol/O_3 rate constant using Environmental Protection Agency's rate constant calculation software, AOPWIN v1.91 is 4.3×10^{-16} cm^3 $molecule^{-1}s^{-1}$ (US Environmental Protection Agency, 2000) is approximately 2 times faster than the experimentally determined value of $2.4 \pm 0.1 \times 10^{-16}$ cm^3 $molecule^{-1}$ s^{-1}.

For the citronellol/OH reaction the experimental parameters were set to minimize other side reactions and highlight the first OH hydrogen abstraction and OH addition step. The citronellol concentration was kept low and the photolysis times were as short as possible. Additionally, nitric oxide (NO) was added to facilitate the generation of OH and to minimize O_3 and NO_3 radical formation preventing other possible radical reactions. The possible mechanistic steps leading to product formation are described below.

Depending on the nature of the radicals formed in Reactions (1) and (4), some reaction products may be formed by multiple pathways.

Acetone

The citronellol/OH reaction mechanism has several potential pathways leading to acetone ($O{=}C(CH_3)_2$) formation. OH can react with citronellol by addition to the double bond, as seen in Fig. 7.2. If OG attaches to carbon (C6), this will leave a radical at carbon (C7). Subsequent addition of oxygen to the (C7). Subsequent addition of oxygen to the (C7) radical results in the dissociation of the $OHCH(\bullet)(CH_2)_2CH(CH_3)(CH_2)_2OH$ radical leaving the peroxyradical, $COO(\bullet)(CH_3)_2$. The $COO(\bullet)(CH_3)_2$ radical can then react with NO to form NO_2 and acetone. This reaction is reasonable, since the AOPWIN calculations indicate that OH addition to the double bond accounts for 88% of citronellol's OH rate constant.

Acetone product formation from the citronellol/O_3 reaction is similar to that of the citronellol/OH reaction, except that acetone may be formed by two different processes in the same scheme. Ozone adds across the double bond to form a primary ozonide. Subsequent decomposition can occur on either side of this primary ozonide ultimately yielding acetone and (6-hydroxy-4-methylhexanal) $HC(=O)(CH_2)_2CH(CH_3)(CH_2)_2OH$.

6-Hydroxy-4-methyhexanal

The chromatographic peak proposed to be 6-hydroxy-4-methylhexanal based on mass spectral data was the largest product peak observed in the PFBHA derivatization experiments from the citronellol/OH and citronellol/O_3 reactions. In the citronellol/OH reaction, 6-hydroxy-4-methylhexanal is likely formed from OH addition to site I, as seen in Fig. 7.2. OH can add to either side of the double bond. If OH adds to carbon (C_6), the resulting product is the radical, $(CH_3)_2C\ (\bullet)\ CH(OH)\ (CH_2)_2CH(CH)_3)(CH_2)_2OH$.

Subsequent addition of oxygen to the radical leads to decomposition and formation of the peroxyradical, $(CH_3)_2COO\bullet$ and the radical, $OHCH(\bullet)(CH_2)_2CH(CH_3)(CH_2)_2OH$. This radical reacts with O_2 to form HO_2 and 6-hydroxy-4-methylhexanal, $HC(=O)(CH_2)_2CH(CH_3)(CH_2)_2OH$. This product was also formed in the citronellol/O_3 reaction as described in the acetone section (above).

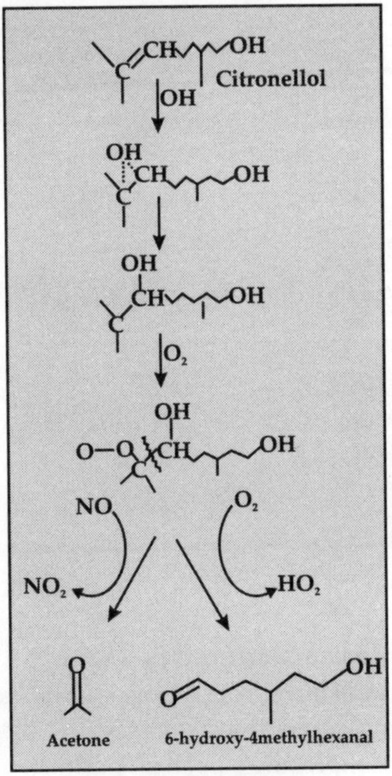

Fig. 7.2: **Reaction mechanism for citronellol + OH showing formation of acetone and 6-hydroxy-4-methylhexanal**

The reaction products: acetone, ethanedial, 2-oxopropanal, and 6-hydroxy-4-methyl-hexanal appear in both the citronellol/OH and the citro-nellol/O_3 reactions, Ozone/alkene reactions can produce steady state OH radical concentrations which would explain the observation of these products in both reactions (Paulson et al., 1999). However, by addition of a large concentration of cyclohexane (410 ppm) in the citronellol/O_3 reaction (which scavenges OH radicals) the citronellol/OH side-reaction is effectively eliminated.

8

Mass Spectrometry

Mass spectrometry (MS) is an analytical technique for the determination of the elemental composition of a sample or molecule. It is also used for elucidating the chemical structures of molecules, such as peptides and other chemical compounds. The MS principle consists of ionizing chemical compounds to generate charged molecules or molecule fragments and measurement of their mass-to-charge ratios. In a typical MS procedure:

- a sample is loaded onto the MS instrument; and
- the components of the sample ionized by one of a variety of methods (e.g., by impacting them with an electron beam), which results in the formation of charged particles (ions);
- directing the ions into a electric and/or magnetic fields;
- computation of the mass-to-charge ratio of the particles based on the details of their motion of the ions as they transit through electromagnetic fields; and

- detection of the ions, which in step 4 were sorted according to m/z.

The MS instruments consist of three modules: an *ion source*, which can convert gas phase sample molecules into ions (or, in the case of electrospray ionization, move ions that exist in solution into the gas phase); a *mass analyzer*, which sorts the ions by their masses by applying electromagnetic fields; and a *detector*, which measures the value of an indicator quantity and thus provides data for calculating the abundances of each ion present. The technique has both qualitative and quantitative uses. These include identifying unknown compounds, determining the isotopic composition of elements in a molecule, and determining the structure of a compound by observing its fragmentation. Other uses include quantifying the amount of a compound in a sample or studying the fundamentals of gas phase ion chemistry (the chemistry of ions and neutrals in a vacuum). The MS is now in very common use in analytical laboratories that study physical, chemical, or biological properties of a great variety of compounds.

Etymology

The word *spectrograph* has been used since 1884 as an *"International Scientific Vocabulary"*. The linguistic roots are a combination and removal of bound morphemes and free morphemes which relate to the terms *spectr-um* and *phot-ograph-ic plate.* Early *spectrometry* devices that measured the mass-to-charge ratio of ions were called *mass spectrographs* which consisted of instruments that recorded a spectrum of mass values on a photographic plate A *mass spectroscope* is similar to a *mass spectrograph* except that the beam of ions is directed onto a phosphor screen A mass spectroscope configuration was used in early instruments when it was desired that the effects of adjustments be quickly observed. Once the instrument was properly adjusted, a photographic plate was inserted and exposed. The term mass spectroscope continued to be used even though the direct illumination of a phosphor screen was replaced by indirect measurements with an oscilloscope. The use of the term *mass spectroscopy* is now discouraged due to the possibility of confusion with light spectroscopy. Mass spectrometry is often abbreviated as *mass-spec* or simply as *MS* Thomson has also noted that a *mass spectroscope* is similar to a *mass spectrograph* except that the beam of ions is directed onto a phosphor screen. The suffix -scope here denotes the direct viewing of the spectra (range) of masses.

History

In 1886, Eugen Goldstein observed rays in gas discharges under low pressure that traveled away from the anode and through channels in a perforated cathode, opposite to the direction of negatively charged cathode rays (which travel from cathode to anode). Goldstein called these positively charged anode rays "Kanalstrahlen"; the standard translation of this term into English is "canal rays". Wilhelm Wien found that strong electric or magnetic fields deflected the canal rays and, in 1899, constructed a device with parallel electric and magnetic fields that separated the positive rays according to their charge-to-mass ratio (Q/m). Wien found that the charge-to-mass ratio depended on the nature of the gas in the discharge tube. English scientist J.J. Thomson later improved on the work of Wien by reducing the pressure to create a mass spectrograph.

Some of the modern techniques of mass spectrometry were devised by Arthur Jeffrey Dempster and F.W. Aston in 1918 and 1919 respectively. In 1989, half of the Nobel Prize in Physics was awarded to Hans Dehmelt and Wolfgang Paul for the development of the ion trap technique in the 1950s and 1960s. In 2002, the Nobel Prize in Chemistry was awarded to John Bennett Fenn for the development of electrospray ionization (ESI) and Koichi Tanaka for the development of soft laser desorption (SLD) in 1987. However earlier, matrix-assisted laser desorption/ionization (MALDI), was developed by Franz Hillenkamp and Michael Karas; this technique has been widely used for protein analysis.

Simplified Example

The following example describes the operation of a spectrometer mass analyzer, which is of the sector type. Consider a sample of sodium chloride (table salt). In the ion source, the sample is vaporized (turned into gas) and ionized (transformed into electrically charged particles) into sodium (Na^+) and chloride (Cl^-) ions. Sodium atoms and ions are monoisotopic, with a mass of about 23 amu. Chloride atoms and ions come in two isotopes with masses of approximately 35 amu (at a natural abundance of about 75 per cent) and approximately 37 amu (at a natural abundance of about 25 percent). The analyzer part of the spectrometer contains electric and magnetic fields, which exert forces on ions traveling through these fields. The speed of a charged particle may be increased or decreased while passing through the electric field, and its direction may be altered by the magnetic field. The magnitude of the deflection of the moving ion's trajectory depends on its mass-to-charge ratio. By Newton's second law of motion, lighter ions get deflected by the magnetic force more than heavier ions. The streams of sorted ions pass from the analyzer to the detector, which records the relative abundance of each ion type. This information is used to determine the chemical element composition of the original sample (i.e. that both sodium and chlorine are present in the sample) and the isotopic composition of its constituents (the ratio of ^{35}Cl to ^{37}Cl).

Instrumentation

Ion Source Technologies

The ion source is the part of the mass spectrometer that ionizes the material under analysis (the analyte). The ions are then transported by magnetic or electric fields to the mass analyzer.

Techniques for ionization have been key to determining what types of samples can be analyzed by mass spectrometry. Electron ionization and *chemical ionization* are used for gases and vapors. In chemical ionization sources, the analyte is ionized by chemical ion-molecule reactions during collisions in the source. Two techniques often used with liquid and solid biological samples include *electrospray ionization* (invented by John Fenn) and matrix-assisted laser desorption/ionization (MALDI).

Inductively coupled plasma (ICP) sources are used primarily for cation analysis of a wide array of sample types. In this type of Ion Source Technology, a 'flame' of plasma that is electrically neutral overall, but that has had a substantial fraction of its atoms ionised by high temperature) is used to atomize introduced sample molecules and to further strip the outer electrons from those atoms. The plasma is usually generated from argon gas, since the first ionization energy of argon atoms is higher than the first of any other elements except He, O, F and Ne, but lower than the second ionization energy of all except the most electropositive metals. The heating is achieved by a radio-frequency current passed through a coil surrounding the plasma.

Others include glow discharge, field desorption (FD), fast atom bombardment (FAB), thermospray, desorption/ionization on silicon (DIOS), Direct Analysis in Real Time (DART), atmospheric pressure chemical ionization (APCI), secondary ion mass spectrometry (SIMS), spark ionization and thermal ionization (TIMS). Ion Attachment Ionization is a newer soft ionization technique that allows for fragmentation free analysis.

Mass Analyzer Technologies

Mass analyzers separate the ions according to their mass-to-charge ratio. The following two laws govern the dynamics of charged particles in electric and magnetic fields in vacuum:

$\mathbf{F} = Q(\mathbf{E} + \mathbf{v} \times \mathbf{B})$ (Lorentz force law);

$\mathbf{F} = m\mathbf{a}$ (Newton's second law of motion in non-relativistic case, i.e. valid only at ion velocity much lower than the speed of light).

Here **F** is the force applied to the ion, *m* is the mass of the ion, **a** is the acceleration, *Q* is the ion charge, **E** is the electric field, and **v** x **B** is the vector cross product of the ion velocity and the magnetic field.

Equating the above expressions for the force applied to the ion yields:

$(m/Q)\mathbf{a} = \mathbf{E} + \mathbf{v} \times \mathbf{B}$

This differential equation is the classic equation of motion for charged particles. Together with the particle's initial conditions, it completely determines the particle's motion in space and time in terms of *m/Q*. Thus mass spectrometers could be thought of as "mass-to-charge spectrometers". When presenting data, it is common to use the (officially) dimensionless *m/z*, where z is the number of elementary charges (*e*) on the ion (z=Q/e). This quantity, although it is informally called the mass-to-charge ratio, more accurately speaking represents the ratio of the mass number and the charge number, *z*.

There are many types of mass analyzers, using either static or dynamic fields, and magnetic or electric fields, but all operate according to the above differential equation. Each analyzer type has its strengths and weaknesses. Many mass spectrometers use two or more mass analyzers for tandem mass spectrometry (MS/MS). In addition to the more common mass analyzers listed below, there are others designed for special situations.

Sector

A sector field mass analyzer uses an electric and/or magnetic field to affect the path and/or velocity of the charged particles in some way. As shown above, sector instruments bend the trajectories of the ions as they pass through the mass analyzer, according to their mass-to-charge ratios, deflecting the more charged and faster-moving, lighter ions more. The analyzer can be used to select a narrow range of *m/z* or to scan through a range of *m/z* to catalog the ions present.

Time-of-flight

The time-of-flight (TOF) analyzer uses an electric field to accelerate the ions through the same potential, and then measures the time they take to reach the detector. If the particles all have the same charge, the kinetic energies will be identical, and their velocities will depend only on their masses. Lighter ions will reach the detector first.

Quadrupole

Quadrupole mass analyzers use oscillating electrical fields to selectively stabilize or destabilize the paths of ions passing through a radio frequency (RF) quadrupole field. Only a single mass/charge ratio is passed through the system at any time, but changes to the potentials on magnetic lenses allows a wide range of m/z values to be swept rapidly, either continuously or in a succession of discrete hops. A quadrupole mass analyzer acts as a mass-selective filter and is closely related to the Quadrupole ion trap, particularly the linear quadrupole ion trap except that it is designed to pass the untrapped ions rather than collected the trapped ones, and is for that reason referred to as a transmission quadrupole. A common variation of the quadrupole is the triple quadrupole. Triple quadrupole mass spectrometers have three quadrupoles arranged parallel to incoming ions. The first quadrupole acts as a mass filter. The second quadrupole acts as a collision cell where selected ions are broken into fragments. The resulting fragments are scanned by the third quadrupole.

Quadrupole Ion Trap

The quadrupole ion trap works on the same physical principles as the quadrupole mass analyzer, but the ions are trapped and sequentially ejected. Ions are created and trapped in a mainly quadrupole RF potential and separated by m/Q, non-destructively or destructively.

There are many mass/charge separation and isolation methods but most commonly used is the mass instability mode in which the RF potential is ramped so that the orbit of ions with a mass $a > b$ are stable while ions with mass b become unstable and are ejected on the z-axis onto a detector.

Ions may also be ejected by the resonance excitation method, whereby a supplemental oscillatory excitation voltage is applied to the endcap electrodes, and the trapping voltage amplitude and/or excitation voltage frequency is varied to bring ions into a resonance condition in order of their mass/charge ratio.

The cylindrical ion trap mass spectrometer is a derivative of the quadrupole ion trap mass spectrometer.

Linear Quadrupole Ion Trap

A linear quadrupole ion trap is similar to a quadrupole ion trap, but it traps ions in a two dimensional quadrupole field, instead of a three dimensional quadrupole field as in a quadrupole ion trap. Thermo Fisher's LTQ ("linear trap quadrupole") is an example of the linear ion trap.

Fourier Transform Ion Cyclotron Resonance

Fourier transform mass spectrometry, or more precisely Fourier transform ion cyclotron resonance MS, measures mass by detecting the image current produced by ions cyclotroning in the presence of a magnetic field. Instead of measuring the deflection of ions with a detector such as an electron multiplier, the ions are injected into a Penning trap (a static electric/ magnetic ion trap) where they effectively form part of a circuit. Detectors at fixed positions in space measure the electrical signal of ions which pass near them over time, producing a periodic signal. Since the frequency of an ion's cycling is determined by its mass to charge ratio, this can be deconvoluted by performing a Fourier transform on the signal. FTMS has the advantage of high sensitivity (since each ion is "counted" more than once) and much higher resolution and thus precision

Ion cyclotron resonance (ICR) is an older mass analysis technique similar to FTMS except that ions are detected with a traditional detector. Ions trapped in a Penning trap are excited by an RF electric field until they impact the wall of the trap, where the detector is located. Ions of different mass are resolved according to impact time.

Orbitrap

Very similar nonmagnetic FTMS has been performed, where ions are electrostatically trapped in an orbit around a central, spindle shaped electrode. The electrode confines the ions so that they both orbit around the central electrode and oscillate back and forth along the central electrode's long axis. This oscillation generates an image current in the detector plates which is recorded by the instrument. The frequencies of these image currents depend on the mass to charge ratios of the ions. Mass spectra are obtained by Fourier transformation of the recorded image currents.

Similar to Fourier transform ion cyclotron resonance mass spectrometers, Orbitraps have a high mass accuracy, high sensitivity and a good dynamic range.

Detector

The final element of the mass spectrometer is the detector. The detector records either the charge induced or the current produced when an ion passes by or hits a surface. In a scanning instrument, the signal produced in the detector during the course of the scan versus where the instrument is in the scan (at what m/Q) will produce a mass spectrum, a record of ions as a function of m/Q.

Typically, some type of electron multiplier is used, though other detectors including Faraday cups and ion-to-photon detectors are also used. Because the number of ions leaving the mass analyzer at a particular instant is typically quite small, considerable amplification is often necessary to get a signal. Microchannel Plate Detectors are commonly used in modern commercial instruments] In FTMS and Orbitraps, the detector consists of a pair of metal surfaces within the mass analyzer/ion trap region which the ions only pass near as they oscillate. No DC current is produced, only a weak AC image current is produced in a circuit between the electrodes. Other inductive detectors have also been used.

Tandem Mass Spectrometry

A tandem mass spectrometer is one capable of multiple rounds of mass spectrometry, usually separated by some form of molecule fragmentation. For example, one mass analyzer can isolate one peptide from many entering a mass spectrometer. A second mass analyzer then stabilizes the peptide ions while they collide with a gas, causing them to fragment by collision-induced dissociation (CID). A third mass analyzer then sorts the fragments produced from the peptides. Tandem MS can also be done in a single mass analyzer over time, as in a quadrupole ion trap. There are various methods for fragmenting molecules for tandem MS, including collision-induced dissociation (CID), electron capture dissociation (ECD), electron transfer dissociation (ETD), infrared multiphoton dissociation (IRMPD) and blackbody infrared radiative dissociation (BIRD). An important application using tandem mass spectrometry is in protein identification.

Tandem mass spectrometry enables a variety of experimental sequences. Many commercial mass spectrometers are designed to expedite the execution of such routine sequences as single reaction monitoring (SRM), multiple reaction monitoring (MRM), and precursor ion scan. In SRM, the first analyzer allows only a single mass through and the second analyzer monitors for a single user defined fragment ion. MRM allows for multiple user defined fragment ions. SRM and MRM are most often used with scanning instruments where the second mass analysis event is duty cycle limited. These experiments are used to increase specificity of detection of known molecules, notably in pharmacokinetic studies. Precursor ion scan refers to monitoring for a specific loss from the precursor ion. The first and second mass analyzers scan across the spectrum as partitioned by a user defined *m/z* value. This experiment is used to detect specific motifs within unknown molecules.

An important type of Tandem mass spectrometry is Accelerator Mass Spectrometry (AMS), which uses very high voltages, usually in the mega-volt range, to accelerate negative ions into a type of tandem mass spectrometer. One of the most important applications of this technique is radiocarbon dating.

Common Mass Spectrometer Configurations and Techniques

When a specific configuration of source, analyzer, and detector becomes conventional in practice, often a compound acronym arises to designate it, and the compound acronym may be more well known among nonspectrometrists than the component acronyms. The epitome of this is MALDI-TOF, which simply refers to combining a matrix-assisted laser desorption/ ionization source with a time-of-flight mass analyzer. The MALDI-TOF moniker is more widely recognized by the non-mass spectrometrist scientist than MALDI or TOF individually. Other examples include inductively coupled plasma-mass spectrometry (ICP-MS), accelerator mass spectrometry (AMS), Thermal ionization-mass spectrometry (TIMS) and spark source mass spectrometry (SSMS). Sometimes the use of the generic "MS" actually connotes a very specific mass analyzer and detection system, as is the case with AMS, which is always sector based.

Certain applications of mass spectrometry have developed monikers that although strictly speaking they would seem to refer to a broad application, in practice have come instead to connote a specific or a limited number of instrument configurations. An example of this is isotope ratio mass spectrometry (IRMS), which refers in practice to the use of a limited number of sector based mass analyzers; this name is used to refer to both the application and the instrument used for the application.

Chromatographic Techniques Combined with Mass Spectrometry

An important enhancement to the mass resolving and mass determining capabilities of mass spectrometry is using it in tandem with chromatographic separation techniques.

Gas Chromatography

A common combination is gas chromatography-mass spectrometry (GC/MS or GC-MS). In this technique, a gas chromatograph is used to separate different compounds. This stream of separated compounds is fed online into the ion source, a metallic filament to which voltage is applied. This filament emits electrons which ionize the compounds. The ions can then further fragment, yielding predictable patterns. Intact ions and fragments pass into the mass spectrometer's analyzer and are eventually detected.

Liquid Chromatography

Similar to gas chromatography MS (GC/MS), liquid chromatography mass spectrometry (LC/MS or LC-MS) separates compounds chromatographically before they are introduced to the ion source and mass spectrometer. It differs from GC/MS in that the mobile phase is liquid, usually a mixture of water and organic solvents, instead of gas. Most commonly, an electrospray ionization source is used in LC/MS. There are also some newly developed ionization techniques like laser spray.

Ion Mobility

Ion mobility spectrometry/mass spectrometry (IMS/MS or IMMS) is a technique where ions are first separated by drift time through some neutral gas under an applied electrical potential gradient before being introduced into a mass spectrometer. Drift time is a measure of the radius relative to the charge of the ion. The duty cycle of IMS (the time over which the experiment takes place) is longer than most mass spectrometric techniques, such that the mass spectrometer can sample along the course of the IMS separation. This produces data about the IMS separation and the mass-to-charge ratio of the ions in a manner similar to LC/MS.

The duty cycle of IMS is short relative to liquid chromatography or gas chromatography separations and can thus be coupled to such techniques, producing triple modalities such as LC/IMS/MS.

Applications

Mass spectrometry is also used to determine the isotopic composition of elements within a sample. Differences in mass among isotopes of an element are very small, and the less abundant isotopes of an element are typically very rare, so a very sensitive instrument is required. These instruments, sometimes referred to as isotope ratio mass spectrometers (IR-MS), usually use a single magnet to bend a beam of ionized particles towards a series of Faraday cups which convert particle impacts to electric current. A fast on-line analysis of deuterium content of water can be done using Flowing afterglow mass spectrometry, FA-MS. Probably the most sensitive and accurate mass spectrometer for this purpose is the accelerator mass spectrometer (AMS). Isotope ratios are important markers of a variety of processes. Some isotope ratios are used to determine the age of materials for example as in carbon dating. Labelling with stable isotopes is also used for protein quantification.

Trace Gas Analysis

Several techniques use ions created in a dedicated ion source injected into a flow tube or a drift tube: selected ion flow tube (SIFT-MS), and proton transfer reaction (PTR-MS), are variants of chemical ionization dedicated for trace gas analysis of air, breath or liquid headspace using well defined reaction time allowing calculations of analyte concentrations from the known reaction kinetics without the need for internal standard or calibration.

Atom Probe

An atom probe is an instrument that combines time-of-flight mass spectrometry and field ion microscopy (FIM) to map the location of individual atoms.

Pharmacokinetics

Pharmacokinetics is often studied using mass spectrometry because of the complex nature of the matrix (often blood or urine) and the need for high sensitivity to observe low dose and long time point data. The most common instrumentation used in this application is LC-MS with a triple quadrupole mass spectrometer. Tandem mass spectrometry is usually employed for added specificity. Standard curves and internal standards are used for quantitation of usually a single pharmaceutical in the samples. The samples represent different time points as a pharmaceutical is administered and then metabolized or cleared from the body. Blank or t=0 samples taken before administration are important in determining background and insuring data integrity with such complex sample matrices. Much attention is paid to the linearity of the standard curve; however it is not uncommon to use curve fitting with more complex functions such as quadratics since the response of most mass spectrometers is less than linear across large concentration ranges.

There is currently considerable interest in the use of very high sensitivity mass spectrometry for microdosing studies, which are seen as a promising alternative to animal experimentation.

Protein Characterization

Mass spectrometry is an important emerging method for the characterization of proteins. The two primary methods for ionization of whole proteins are electrospray ionization (ESI) and matrix-assisted laser desorption/ ionization (MALDI). In keeping with the performance and mass range of available mass spectrometers, two approaches are used for characterizing proteins. In the first, intact proteins are ionized by either of the two techniques described above, and then introduced to a mass analyser. This approach is referred to as "top-down" strategy of protein analysis. In the second, proteins are enzymatically digested into smaller peptides using proteases such as trypsin or pepsin, either in solution or in gel after electrophoretic separation. Other proteolytic agents are also used. The collection of peptide products are then introduced to the mass analyser. When the characteristic pattern of peptides is used for the identification of the protein the method is called peptide mass fingerprinting (PMF), if the identification is performed using the sequence data determined in tandem MS analysis it is called de novo sequencing. These procedures of protein analysis are also referred to as the "bottom-up" approach.

Space Exploration

As a standard method for analysis, mass spectrometers have reached other planets and moons. Two were taken to Mars by the Viking program. In early 2005 the Cassini-Huygens mission delivered a specialized GC-MS instrument aboard the Huygens probe through the atmosphere of Titan, the largest moon of the planet Saturn. This instrument analyzed atmospheric samples along its descent trajectory and was able to vaporize and analyze samples of Titan's frozen, hydrocarbon covered surface once the probe had landed. These measurements compare the abundance of isotope(s) of each particle comparatively to earth's natural abundance. Also onboard the Cassini-Huygens spacecraft is an ion and neutral mass spectrometer which has been taking measurements of Titan's atmospheric composition as well as the composition of Enceladus' plumes.

Mass spectrometers are also widely used in space missions to measure the composition of plasmas. For example, the Cassini spacecraft carries the Cassini Plasma Spectrometer (CAPS) which measures the mass of ions in Saturn's magnetosphere.

Respired Gas Monitor

Mass spectrometers were used in hospitals for respiratory gas analysis beginning around 1975 through the end of the century. Some are probably still in use but none are currently being manufactured.

Found mostly in the operating room, they were a part of a complex system in which respired gas samples from patients undergoing anesthesia were drawn into the instrument through a valve mechanism designed to sequentially connect up to 32 rooms to the mass spectrometer. A computer directed all operations of the system. The data collected from the mass spectrometer was delivered to the individual rooms for the anesthesiologist to use.

This magnetic sector mass spectrometer's uniqueness may have been the fact that a plane of detectors, each purposely positioned to collect all of the ion species expected to be in the samples, allowed the instrument to simultaneously report all of the patient respired gases. Although the mass range was limited to slightly over 120 u, fragmentation of some of the heavier molecules negated the need for a higher detection limit.

PHASE (MATTER)

In the physical sciences, a phase is a region of space (a thermodynamic system), throughout which all physical properties of a material are essentially uniform Examples of physical properties include density, index of refraction, and chemical composition. A simple description is that a phase is a region of material that is chemically uniform, physically distinct, and (often) mechanically separable. In a system consisting of ice and water in a glass jar, the ice cubes are one phase, the water is a second phase, and the humid air over the water is a third phase. The glass of the jar is another separate phase.

The term 'phase' is sometimes used as a synonym for state of matter. Also, the term phase is sometimes used to refer to a set of equilibrium states demarcated in terms of state variables such as pressure and temperature by a phase boundary on a phase diagram. Because phase boundaries relate to changes in the organization of matter, such as a change from liquid to solid or a more subtle change from one crystal structure to another, this latter usage is similar to the use of "phase" as a synonym for state of matter. However, the state of matter and phase diagram usages are not commensurate with the formal definition given above and the intended meaning must be determined in part from the context in which the term is used.

Types of Phases

Distinct phases may be described as different states of matter such as gas, liquid, solid, plasma or Bose–Einstein condensate. Phases may also be differentiated based on solubility as in polar (hydrophilic) or non-polar (hydrophobic). A mixture of water (a polar liquid) and oil (a non-polar liquid) will spontaneously separate into two phases. Water has a very low solubility (is insoluble) in oil and oil has a low solubility in water. Solubility is the maximum amount of a solute that can dissolve in a solvent before the solute ceases to dissolve and remains in a separate phase. A mixture can separate into more than two liquid phases and the concept of phase separation extends to solids, i.e. solids can form solid solutions or crystallize into distinct crystal phases. Metal pairs that are mutually soluble can form alloys, whereas metal pair that are mutually insoluble cannot.

As many as eight immiscible liquid phases have been observed Mutually immiscible liquid phases are formed from water (aqueous phase), hydrophobic organic solvents, perfluorocarbons (fluorous phase), silicones, several different metals, and also from molten phosphorus. Not all organic solvents are completely miscible, e.g. a mixture of ethylene glycol and toluene may separate into two distinct organic phases Emulsions and colloids are examples of immiscible phase pair combinations that do not physically separate.

Phase Equilibrium

Left to equilibrate, many compositions will form a uniform single phase, but depending on the temperature and pressure even a single substance may separate into two or more distinct phases. Within each phase, the properties are uniform but between the two phase properties differ.

Water in a closed jar with an air space over it forms a two phase system. Most of the water is in the liquid phase, where it is held by the mutual attraction of water molecules. Even at equilibrium molecules are constantly in motion and, once in a while, a molecule in the liquid phase gains enough kinetic energy to break away from the liquid phase and enter the gas phase. Likewise, every once in a while a vapor molecule collides with the liquid surface and condenses into the liquid. At equilibrium, evaporation and condensation processes exactly balance and there is no net change in the volume of either phase.

At room temperature and pressure, the water jar reaches equilibrium when the air over the water has a humidity of about 3%. This percentage increases as the temperature goes up. At 100 C and atmospheric pressure, equilibrium is not reached until the air is 100% water. If the liquid is heated a little over 100 C, the transition from liquid to gas will occur not only at the surface, but throughout the liquid volume: the water boils.

Number of Phases

For a given composition, only certain phases are possible at a given temperature and pressure. The number and type of phases that will form is hard to predict and is usually determined by experiment. The results of such experiments can be plotted in phase diagrams.

The phase diagram shown here is for a single component system. In this simple system, which phases that are possible depends only on pressure and temperature. The markings show points where two or more phases can co-exist in equilibrium. At temperatures and pressures away from the markings, there will be only one phase at equilibrium.

In the Fig. 8.1, the blue line marking the boundary between liquid and gas does not continue indefinitely, but terminates at a point called the critical point. As the temperature and pressure approach the critical point, the properties of the liquid and gas become progressively more similar. At the critical point, the liquid and gas become indistinguishable. Above the critical point, there are no longer separate liquid and gas phases: there is only a generic fluid phase referred to as a supercritical fluid. In water, the critical point occurs at around 647 K (374 °C or 705 °F) and 22.064 MPa.

An unusual feature of the water phase diagram that the solid-liquid phase line (illustrated by the dotted green line) has a negative slope. For most substances, the slope is positive as exemplified by the dark green line. This unusual feature of water is related to ice having a lower density than liquid water. Increasing the pressure drives the water into the higher density phase, which causes melting.

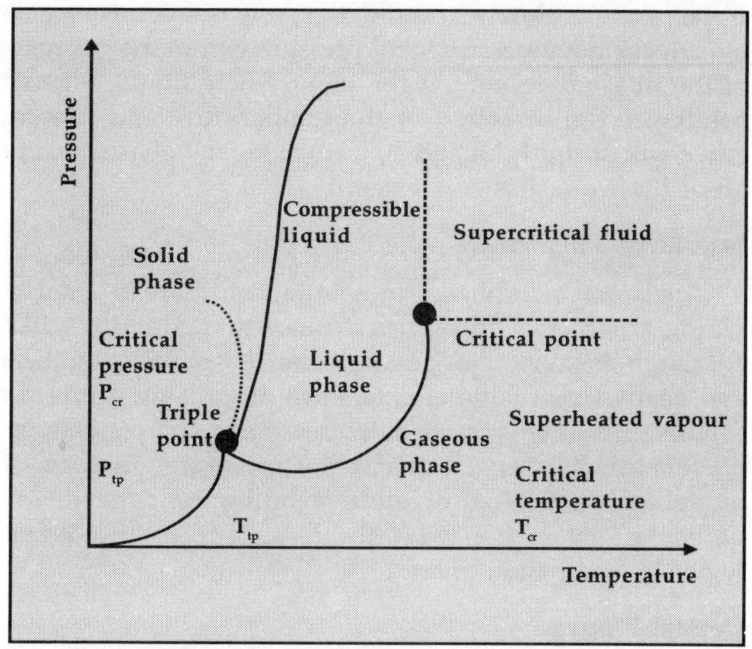

Fig 8.1: **A typical phase diagram for a single-component material, exhibiting solid, liquid and gaseous phases. The solid green line shows the usual shape of the liquid-solid phase line. The dotted green line shows the anomalous behaviour of water**

Another interesting though not unusual feature of the phase diagram is the point where the solid-liquid phase line meets the liquid-gas phase line. The intersection is referred to as the triple point. At the triple point, all three phases can coexist.

Experimentally, the phase lines are relatively easy to map due to the interdependence of temperature and pressure that develops when multiple phases forms. See Gibbs' phase rule. Consider a test apparatus consisting of a closed and well insulated cylinder equipped with a piston. By charging the right amount of water and applying heat, the system can be brought to any point in the gas region of the phase diagram.

If the piston is slowly lowered, the system will trace a curve of increasing temperature and pressure within the gas region of the phase diagram. At the point where liquid begins to condense, the direction of the temperature and pressure curve will abruptly change to trace along the phase line until all of the water has condensed.

Interfacial Phenomena

Between two phases in equilibrium there is a narrow region where the properties are not that of either phase. Although this region may be very thin, it can have significant and easily observable effects, such as causing a liquid to exhibit surface tension. In mixtures, some components may preferentially move toward the interface. In terms of modeling, describing, or understanding the behavior of a particular system, it may be efficacious to treat the interfacial region as a separate phase.

Crystal Phases

A single material may have several distinct solid states capable of forming separate phases. Water is a well known example of such a material. For example, water ice is ordinarily found in the hexagonal form Ice Ih, but can also exist as the cubic ice Ic, the rhombohedral ice II, and many other forms. Polymorphism is the ability of a solid to exist in more than one crystal form. For pure chemical elements, polymorphism is known as allotropy. For example, diamond, graphite, and fullerenes are different allotropes of carbon.

Phase Transitions

When a substance undergoes a phase transition (changes from one state of matter to another) it usually either takes up or releases energy. For example, when water evaporates, the kinetic energy expended as the evaporating molecules escape the attractive forces of the liquid is reflected in a decrease in temperature. The amount of energy required to induce the transition is more than the amount required to heat the water from room temperature to just short of boiling temperature, which is why evaporation is useful for cooling. See Enthalpy of vaporization. The reverse process, condensation, releases heat. The heat energy, or enthalpy, associated with a solid to liquid transition is the enthalpy of fusion and that associated with a solid to gas transition is the enthalpy of sublimation.

9

Gas-Liquid Chromatography

Gas-liquid chromatography (often just called gas chromatography) is a powerful tool in analysis. It has all sorts of variations in the way it is done - if you want full details, a Google search on gas chromatography will give you scary amounts of information if you need it! This page just looks in a simple introductory way at how it can be carried out.

Carrying out Gas-liquid Chromatography

Introduction

All forms of chromatography involve a *stationary phase* and a *mobile phase*. In all the other forms of chromatography you will meet at this level, the mobile phase is a liquid. In gas-liquid chromatography, the mobile phase is a gas such as helium and the stationary phase is a high boiling point liquid absorbed onto a solid.

How fast a particular compound travels through the machine will depend on how much of its time is spent moving with the gas as opposed to being attached to the liquid in some way.

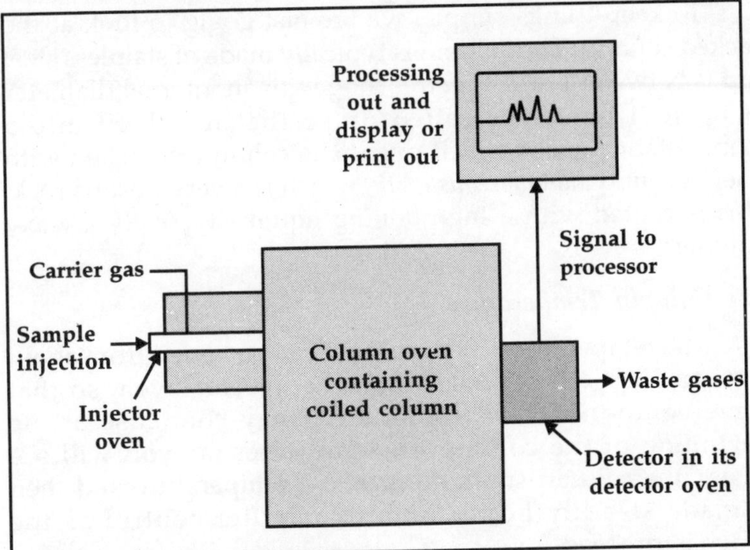

Fig 9.1: **A Flow Scheme for Gas-liquid Chromatography**

Injection of the Sample

Very small quantities of the sample that you are trying to analyse are injected into the machine using a small syringe. The syringe needle passes through a thick rubber disc (known as a septum) which reseals itself again when the syringe is pulled out.

The injector is contained in an oven whose temperature can be controlled. It is hot enough so that all the sample boils and is carried into the column as a gas by the helium (or other carrier gas).

How the Column Works

The Packing Material

There are two main types of column in gas-liquid chromatography. One of these is a long thin tube packed with the stationary phase; the other is even thinner and has the stationary phase bonded to its inner surface.

To keep things simple, we are just going to look at the packed column. The column is typically made of stainless steel and is between 1 and 4 metres long with an internal diameter of up to 4 mm. It is coiled up so that it will fit into a thermostatically controlled oven. The column is packed with finely ground *diatomaceous earth*, which is a very porous rock. This is coated with a high boiling liquid - typically a waxy polymer.

The Column Temperature

The temperature of the column can be varied from about 50°C to 250°C. It is cooler than the injector oven, so that some components of the mixture may condense at the beginning of the column. In some cases, as you will see below, the column starts off at a low temperature and then is made steadily hotter under computer control as the analysis proceeds.

How Separation Eorks on the Column

One of three things might happen to a particular molecule in the mixture injected into the column:

- It may condense on the stationary phase.
- It may dissolve in the liquid on the surface of the stationary phase.
- It may remain in the gas phase.

None of these things is necessarily permanent.

A compound with a boiling point higher than the temperature of the column will obviously tend to condense at the start of the column. However, some of it will evaporate again in the same way that water evaporates on a warm day - even though the temperature is well below 100°C. The chances are that it will then condense again a little further along the column.

Similarly, some molecules may dissolve in the liquid stationary phase Some compounds will be more soluble in the liquid than others. The more soluble ones will spend more of their time absorbed into the stationary phase; the less soluble ones will spend more of their time in the gas. The process where a substance divides itself between two immiscible solvents because it is more soluble in one than the other is known as partition.

Now, you might reasonably argue that a gas such as helium can't really be described as a "solvent". But the term *partition* is still used in gas-liquid chromatography. You can say that a substance partitions itself between the liquid stationary phase and the gas. Any molecule in the substance spends some of its time dissolved in the liquid and some of its time carried along with the gas.

Retention Time

The time taken for a particular compound to travel through the column to the detector is known as its retention time. This time is measured from the time at which the sample is injected to the point at which the display shows a maximum peak height for that compound. Different compounds have different retention times. For a particular compound, the retention time will vary depending on:

- the boiling point of the compound. A compound which boils at a temperature higher than the column temperature is going to spend nearly all of its time condensed as a liquid at the beginning of the column. So high boiling point means a long retention time.
- the solubility in the liquid phase. The more soluble a compound is in the liquid phase, the less time it will spend being carried along by the gas. High solubility in the liquid phase means a high retention time.
- the temperature of the column. A higher temperature will tend to excite molecules into the gas phase - either because they evaporate more readily, or because they are so energetic that the attractions of the liquid no longer hold them. A high column temperature shortens retention times for everything in the column.

For a given sample and column, there isn't much you can do about the boiling points of the compounds or their solubility in the liquid phase - but you do have control over the temperature.

The lower the temperature of the column, the better the separation you will get - but it could take a *very* long time to get the compounds through which are condensing at the beginning of the column!

On the other hand, using a high temperature, everything will pass through the column much more quickly - but less well separated out. If everything passed through in a very short time, there isn't going to be much space between their peaks on the chromatogram.

The answer is to start with the column relatively cool, and then gradually and very regularly increase the temperature.

At the beginning, compounds which spend most of their time in the gas phase will pass quickly through the column and be detected. Increasing the temperature a bit will encourage the slightly "stickier" compounds through. Increasing the temperature still more will force the very "sticky" molecules off the stationary phase and through the column.

The Detector

There are several different types of detector in use. The flame ionisation detector described below is commonly used and is easier to describe and explain than the alternatives.

A Flame Ionisation Detector

In terms of reaction mechanisms, the burning of an organic compound is very complicated. During the process, small amounts of ions and electrons are produced in the flame. The presence of these can be detected.

The whole detector is enclosed in its own oven which is hotter than the column temperature. That stops anything condensing in the detector.

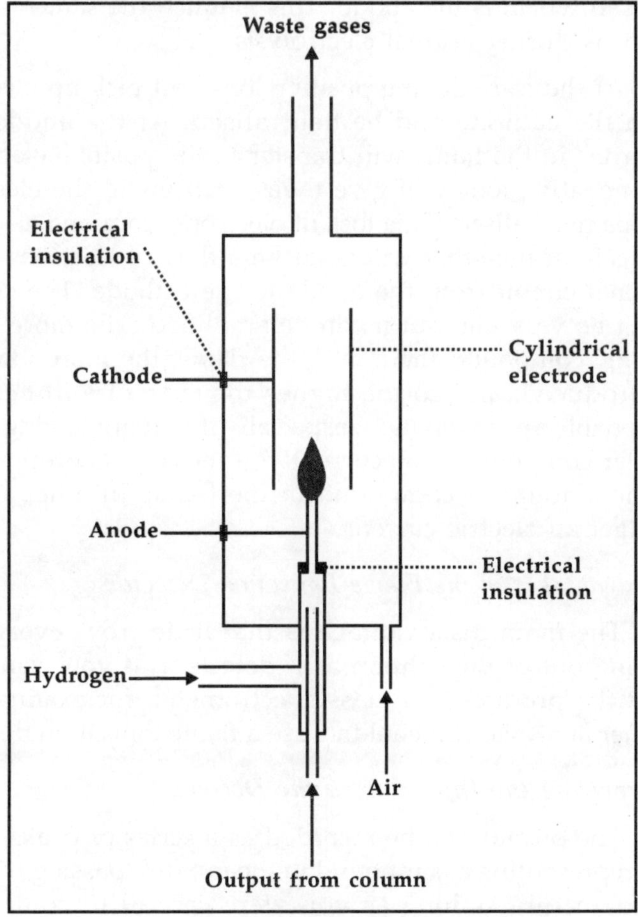

Fig. 9.2: **The flame ionisation detector**

If there is nothing organic coming through from the column, you just have a flame of hydrogen burning in air. Now suppose that one of the compounds in the mixture you are analysing starts to come through. As it burns, it will produce small amounts of ions and electrons in the flame. The positive ions will be attracted to the cylindrical cathode. Negative ions and electrons will be attracted towards the jet itself which is the anode. This is much the same as what happens during normal electrolysis.

At the cathode, the positive ions will pick up electrons from the cathode and be neutralised. At the anode, any electrons in the flame will transfer to the positive electrode; and negative ions will give their electrons to the electrode and be neutralised. This loss of electrons from one electrode and gain at the other will result in a flow of electrons in the external circuit from the anode to the cathode. The current won't be very big, but it can be amplified. The more of the organic compound there is in the flame, the more ions will be produced, and so the higher the current will be. As a reasonable approximation, especially if you are talking about similar compounds, the current you measure is proportional to the amount of compound in the flame. In other words, you get an electric current.

Disadvantages of the Flame Ionisation Detector

The main disadvantage is that it destroys everything coming out of the column as it detects it. If you wanted to send the product to a mass spectrometer, for example, for further analysis, you couldn't use a flame ionisation detector.

Interpreting the Output from the Detector

The output will be recorded as a series of peaks - each one representing a compound in the mixture passing through the detector. As long as you were careful to control the conditions on the column, you could use the retention times to help to identify the compounds present - provided, of course, that you (or somebody else) had already measured them for pure samples of the various compounds under those identical conditions. But you can also use the peaks as a way of measuring the relative quantities of the compounds present.

This is only accurate if you are analysing mixtures of similar compounds - for example, of similar hydrocarbons.

There might be a lot of one compound present, but it might emerge from the column in relatively small amounts over quite a long time. Measuring the area rather than the peak height allows for this.

Coupling a Gas Chromatogram to a Mass Spectrometer

This can't be done with a flame ionisation detector which destroys everything passing through it. Assuming you are using a non-destructive detector . . .

When the detector is showing a peak, some of what is passing through the detector at that time can be diverted to a mass spectrometer. There it will give a fragmentation pattern which can be compared against a computer database of known patterns. That means that the identity of a huge range of compounds can be found without having to know their retention times.

10

Equilibrium

Gas-Phase Equilibrium

Overview of Basic Kinetics

Chemical Kinetics: The study of the rates of chemical reactions.

Rate of a Reaction: The rate at which the reactants are changed into the products of a reaction. The change in concentration of one of the reactants (ΔX), during a given period of time (Δt)

$$\text{Rate of Reaction} = \frac{\Delta X}{\Delta t}$$

Rate Law: A mathematical equation that describes the rate of a chemical reaction. It relates how the rate of a chemical reaction depends on the concentrations of the reactants consumed in that reaction.

$$\text{rate} = k[O_3]$$

- *Rate Constant (k):* The proportionality constant in the rate law equation that describes the relationship between the rate of a step in a chemical reaction and the product of the concentrations of the reactants consumed in that step.

Collision Theory: A model for gas-phase reactions which assumes that molecules must collide in order to react. This helps to explain why the rate of a reaction is proportional to the reactants in a reaction. As a reaction proceeds in the forward direction, reactants are consumed. As the reactants are consumed, the rate of the reaction decreases because there are fewer and fewer molecules available to collide and react.

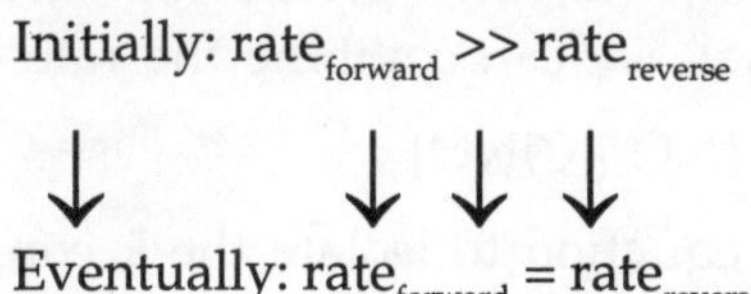

When the rates of the forward and reverse reactions are equal, the reaction will seem like it has stopped. The reactants are being consumed at the same rate that they are being produced, and there seems to be no net change in the concentrations of the reactants and the products. The reaction is at *equilibrium*.

Equilibrium

Equilibrium has a two-part definition

- The point at which there is no longer a changed in the concentrations of the reactants and the products of a chemical reaction.
- The point at which the rates of the forward and reverse reactions are equal.

As was done with the acid-base equilibrium reactions, it is assumed that reactions that strongly favor the products and are not reversible go to completion. This is indicated by a regular forward arrow:

$2\ Mg + O_2 \rightarrow 2\ MgO$

On the other hand, reactions that are reversible and reach equilibrium are written using a forward/backward arrow:

$ClNO_2 + NO \rightleftharpoons NO_2 + ClNO$

Let's follow the equilibrium reaction above. When this system is at equilibrium, by definition, the rates of the forward and reverse reactions are equal. The rate laws for the forward and reverse reactions are:

$rate_{forward} = k_f[ClNO_2][NO]$ and $rate_{reverse} = k_r[NO_2][ClNO]$

Since at equilibrium, the rates of the forward and reverse reactions are equal, we can combine the rate laws:

$k_f[ClNO_2][NO] = k_r\ [NO_2][ClNO]$

If we rearrange the equation to isolate the k constants on one side, we have:

$$\frac{k_f}{k_r} = \frac{[NO_2][ClNO]}{[ClNO_2][NO]}$$

Since the k values are constants, they can be combined to make a single *equilibrium constant* (K_c). The resulting equation is equilibrium constant expression:

$$\frac{k_f}{k_r} = K_c$$

Equilibrium constant expression: The mathematical product of the products of the reaction divided by the mathematical product of the reactants of the reaction:

$$K_c = \frac{[NO_2][ClNO]}{[ClNO_2][NO]}$$

When a reaction reaches equilibrium, the ratio of the concentrations of the products to the concentrations of the reactants as described by the equilibrium constant expression will always be the same (at constant temperature).

How to write equilibrium constant expressions

- In an equilibrium reaction, even though the reaction proceeds in both directions, the reagents to the left of the arrow are assumed to be the reactants and the reagents to the right of the arrow are assumed to be the products. This is just like any non-equilibrium reaction.
- The products are written on top, in the numerator.
- The reactants are written on the bottom in the denominator.
- Each of the products and reactants are raised to an exponent equal to the respective coefficient of each reagent in the balanced reaction.

Sample equilibrium constant expressions:

1. $2\ NO_2(g) \rightleftharpoons N_2O_4(g)$

The product, N_2O_4, goes on the top, and the reactant, NO_2, goes on the bottom. The NO_2 is raised to the second power (squared) since it has a coefficient of 2:

$$K_c = \frac{[N_2O_4]}{[NO_2]^2}$$

2. $2\ SO_3(g) \rightleftharpoons 2\ SO_2(g) + O_2(g)$

The products, SO_2 and O_2, go on the top, and the reactant, SO_3, goes on the bottom. The SO_2 and SO_3 are both raised to the second power (squared) because they both have coefficients of 2:

$$K_c = \frac{[SO_2]^2[O_2]}{[SO_3]^2}$$

3. $N_2(g) + 3\ H_2(g) \rightleftharpoons 2\ NH_3(g)$

The product, NH_3, goes on the top, and the reactants, N_2 and H_2 goes on the bottom. The H_2 is raised to the third power (cubed) since it has a coefficient of 3. The NH_3 is raised to the second power (squared) since it has a coefficient of 2:

$$K_c = \frac{[NH_3]^2}{[N_2][H_2]^3}$$

Reaction Quotient (Qc): The mathematical product of the concentrations of the products of a reaction divided by the mathematical product of the concentrations of the reactants of a reaction at any moment in time. That is, this is basically the equilibrium constant expression, but when the reaction does not necessarily have to be at equilibrium.

The reaction quotient can be used to determine in which direction a system must shift in order to reach equilibrium. There are three possible situations:

1. $Q_c < K_c$: This occurs if there is too much reactant and not enough product. In order to raise Q_c to equilibrium (K_c), some of the reactants must be converted to products, thereby decreasing the denominator and increasing the numerator. In other words, the system must *shift right*.
2. $Q_c = K_c$ - The system is at *Equilibrium*.
3. $Q_c > K_c$ - This occurs if there is too much product and not enough reactant. In order to lower Q_c to equilibrium (K_c), some of the products must be converted back to reactants, thereby decreasing the numerator and increasing the denominator. In other words, the system must *shift left*.

The relative difference between Q_c and K_c indicates also how far a reaction must go to reach equilibrium. If the difference is large, the reaction must shift a lot. If the difference is relatively small, then the reaction will only shift slightly.

Sample Gas-Equilibrium Calculations

The method of solving gas-equilibrium calculations is much like how weak acid calculations are solved.

Check the difference between Q_c and K_c

- If the difference is relatively small, proceed with the problem as follows.
- If the difference is relatively large, the following method will most likely not work.

Set up a Concentration Chart

- Assign Δ as the unknown amount of reactant that is converted to products.
  - Therefore the equilibrium concentration of the reactants is: *initial* - XΔ, where x is the respective coefficients of the reactants.
- XΔ is also the value for the the concentration of the products formed, where x is the respective coefficients of the products

  Write the gas equilibrium constant expression (K_c).

  Substitute

  Assume that Δ is negligible when subtracted.

  Solved for Δ

Check to make sure the assumption was valid

- If the assumption fails then we must solve for Δ by first shifting the reaction completely to the right and coming back to equilibrium by shifting slightly left.

1. $N_{2(g)} + 3H_{2(g)} \rightleftharpoons 2NH_{3(g)}$

Assume the initial concentrations of both N_2 and H_2 are 0.100 M. Calculate the equilibrium concentrations of N_2, H_2, and NH_3 at 500° C if K_c at this temperature is 0.040.

Check the difference between Q_c and K_c. Q_c is initially 0 since no products have been formed yet. 0 < 0.040, but not by a great margin, so it we can proceed with the problem.

Set up the concentration Chart:

- *Note:* Unlike in the weak acid calculations, the reactants and products in the balanced reaction have coefficients which reflect the mole ratios. For every mole of N_2 consumed, 3Δ moles of H_2 must also be consumed, hence the 3. For every mole of N_2 consumed, 2 moles of NH_3 are formed, hence the 2Δ.

	$[N_2]$	$[H_2]$	$[NH_3]$
Initial:	0.100 M	0.100 M	0
Equlibrium:	0.100–Δ	0.100 - 3Δ	2Δ

Set up the *Equilibrium Constant Expression* (Q_c) and *Substitute* in the values from the chart and the given:

$$K_c = \frac{[NH_3]^2}{[H_2]^3[N_2]} \rightarrow 0.040 = \frac{(2\Delta)^2}{(0.100-3\Delta)^3(0.100-\Delta)}$$

Assume that Δ and 3Δ are negligible when subtracted from the initial concentrations of the reactants:

$$\frac{(2\Delta)^2}{(0.100-3\Delta)^3(0.100-\Delta)} = \frac{4\Delta^2}{(0.100)^3(0.100)}$$

Solve for Δ:

$$\frac{4\Delta^2}{(0.100)^3(0.100)} = \frac{4\Delta^2}{(0.100)^4} 0.040$$

$$4\Delta^2 \quad = (0.040)\,(0.100)^4$$

$$\Delta^2 = \frac{(0.040)(0.100)^4}{4}$$

$$\Delta = \sqrt{\frac{(0.040)(0.100)^4}{4}}$$

$\Delta = 0.001$ M

Check to make sure that less than 5% of the reactants were converted to products:

$$\frac{\Delta}{\text{initial}} \times 100 = \frac{0.001\,\text{M}}{0.100\,\text{M}} \times 100 = 1\% < 5\%$$

Since our assumption was valid, we plug Δ back into the values on our chart to find the equilibrium concentrations:

$\Delta = 0.001$ M

$$\begin{array}{lll} [N_2] & = 0.100 - \Delta = 0.100 - 0.001 & = 0.099\ \text{M} \\ [N_2] & = 0.100 - 3\Delta = 0.100 - 3(0.001) & = 0.097\ \text{M} \\ [NH_3] & = 2\Delta = 2\,(0.001) & = 0.002\ \text{M} \end{array}$$

What if the assumption fails?

The above method will generally work for reactions in which the difference between Q_c and K_c is small. That is, the assumption will check out to be valid in the end. If, however, the difference between Q_c and K_c is quite large, then we cannot assume that the reaction will only proceed in the forward direction by a little bit.

$$2\ NO_{(g)} + O_{2(g)} \rightleftharpoons 2\ NO_{2(g)}$$

The initial concentration of NO is 0.100 M and the initial concentration of O_2 is 0.050 M. Calculate the equilibrium concentrations of NO, O_2 and NO_2 if the reaction takes place at 200C and the K_c at this temperature is 3×10^6.

Check the difference between Q_c and K_c. Q_c is initially 0 since no products have been formed yet. 0 is much less than 3×10^6, so we can assume that the reaction has to shift a lot to reach equilibrium. We cannot use the same method used above. Instead we are going to push the reaction all the way to the right so that now there is an intermediate stage where the concentration of the product is 0.100 M (by mole ratio) and the concentrations of the reactants are 0:

	[NO]	$[O_2]$	$[NO_2]$
Initial:	0.100 M	0.050 M	0
Intermediate:	0	0	0.100 M

Now, from the intermediate state, we can set up a chart with the intermediate and equilibrium concentrations. Remember that the coefficients in the balanced reaction are the same coefficients in front of delta according to the mole ratios:

	[NO]	$[O_2]$	$[NO_2]$
Intermediate:	0	0	0.100 M
Equilibrium:	2Δ	Δ	$0.100 - 2\Delta$

Now we can set up the Equilibrium Constant Expression (Q_c) and Substitute in the values from the chart and the given:

$$K_c = \frac{[NO_2]^2}{[NO]^2[O_2]} \rightarrow 3 \times 10^6 = \frac{(0.100 - 2\Delta)^2}{(2\Delta)^2(\Delta)}$$

Assume that 2Δ is negligible when subtracted from the intermediate concentration of the product:

$$\frac{(0.100-2\Delta)^2}{(2\Delta)^2(\Delta)} \rightarrow \frac{(0.100)^2}{(2\Delta)^2(\Delta)}$$

Solve for :

$$\frac{(0.100)^2}{(2\Delta)^2(\Delta)} = 3\times10^6$$

$$4\Delta^3 = \frac{(0.100)^2}{(3\times10^6)}$$

$$\Delta^3 = \frac{(0.100)^2}{(3\times10^6)(4)}$$

$$\Delta = \sqrt[3]{\frac{(0.100)^2}{(3\times10^6)(4)}}$$

$$D = \Delta = 9\times10^{-4}\,\text{M}$$

Check to make sure that less than 5% of the product was converted back to reactants:

$$\frac{\Delta}{\text{intermediate}}\times100 = \frac{9\times10^{-4}\,\text{M}}{0.100\,\text{M}}\times100 = \mathbf{1.8\% < 5\%}$$

Since our assumption was valid, we can find the equilibrium concentrations by plugging in to the values on the chart:

$$\Delta = 9\times10^{-4}\,\text{M} = 0.000\,\text{M}$$

$[NO_2]$ = 0.100 – 2Δ = 0.100 – 2(0.0009) = 0.098 M
$[NO]$ = 2Δ = 2 (0.0009) = 0.0018 M
$[O_2]$ = Δ = 0.0009 M

Gas Equilibrium in Terms of Partial Pressure

Another way to express the gas equilibrium constant expression is with partial pressures of the gases (K_p) in the reaction instead of the concentrations.

$$N_{2(g)} + 3\,H_{2(g)} \rightleftharpoons 2\,NH_{3(g)}$$

For this reaction, the K_c and K_p expressions are:

$$K_c = \frac{[NH_3]^2}{[H_2]^3[N_2]} \text{ and } K_p = \frac{\left(P_{NH_3}\right)^2}{\left(P_{H_2}\right)^3\left(P_{N_2}\right)}$$

The relationship between K_c and K_p is described in the following equation:

$$K_p = K_c \times (RT)^{\Delta n}$$

- R = ideal gas constant = 0.0821 L-atm/mol-K
- T = temperature of the system in Kelvin
- Δn = moles of gas products - moles of gas reactants

Note: When there are equal moles of gas reactants and gas products, n = 0. Any number raised to the 0th power is 1.

Therefore $K_c = K_p$ when the moles of gas products = the moles of gas reactants.

Partial Pressure: The fraction of the total pressure of a mixture of gases that is due to one component of the mixture.

Reaction Quotient (Q_p): The mathematical product of the partial pressures of the products of a reaction divided by the mathematical product of the partial pressures of the reactants of a reaction at any moment in time. This can be used to determine in which direction a reaction will shift to reach equilibrium by comparing the value of Q_p to K_p. Q_p follows the same guidelines as Q_c descrbibed above, just with partial pressures instead of concentrations.

Consider the reaction:

$$N_{2(g)} + 3\,H_{2(g)} \rightleftharpoons 2\,NH_{3(g)}$$

Calculate the Partial Pressures of each of the Gases if the Total Pressure is 2.0 Atom

Calculate the mole fraction of each gas and multiply this by the total pressure to get the partial pressure of each gas The mole fraction of a gas is the moles of the one gas divided by the total moles of gas in the system:

$$P_{N_2} = \frac{1\,\text{mol } N_2}{6\text{ mol total gas}} \times 2.00\text{ atm} = \boxed{0.333\text{ atm}}$$

$$P_{H_2} = \frac{3\text{ mol } H_2}{6\text{ mol total gas}} \times 2.00\text{ atm} = \boxed{1.00\text{ atm}}$$

$$P_{NH_3} = \frac{2\text{ mol } NH_3}{6\text{ mol total gas}} \times 2.00\text{ atm} = \boxed{0.667\text{atm}}$$

Note that the sum of the partial pressures of all the gases equals the total pressure:

$$P_{N_2} + P_{H_2} + P_{NH_3} = \text{Total pressure}$$

$$0.333 + 1.00 + 0.667 = 2.00\text{ atm}$$

Gas Equilibrium Calculations with K_p are solved exactly as K_c problems are solved, just using partial pressures instead of concentrations.

11

Phases and Pressure

Increased pressure increases the range of temperatures over which a substance can exist as a liquid. Reduced pressure reduces this range. At a certain special pressure the boiling and melting points will equal, and the substance can no longer exist as a liquid. Below this pressure, the only possible phase transition is from solid to gas (and *vice versa*). This phase change is called sublimation (the reverse process is called deposition or desublimation) and the temperature at which it occurs is called the sublimation point (or sublimation temperature). That's the essence of the upcoming discussion. If this is enough info for you, stop reading and jump to the next section. Knowing why some phenomena occurs is often more important than knowing that it occurs.

To a certain extent, liquids are like a minimum security prison. (Solids are like a maximum security prison in permanent lock down, but that's another matter.) The molecules within have limited freedom and can only leave infrequently or with great effort. As long as a liquid has some surface area exposed to the atmosphere, here and there a molecule within the liquid near the surface will be moving fast enough to escape the liquid prison and enjoy the freedom of a vapour molecule in the surrounding atmosphere. But rather unlike a a prison, the reverse process is also possible. From time to time, a molecule in the atmosphere will be traveling fast enough to plow its way through the tightly guarded walls of the liquid only to find itself trapped within. Both events are happening simultaneously, but not necessarily with equal probability.

The thing that makes these processes different from inmates entering and leaving a prison is that they aren't so much governed by laws of good or bad behavior, but rather by physical laws describing energy and momentum. If a molecule of a liquid has sufficient momentum in the right direction, it will escape the liquid. Likewise, if a molecule of a vapour has sufficient momentum and is traveling in the wrong direction, it will join the liquid.

Given a droplet of water on the side of a glass; when more molecules of water escape the droplet than enter from the atmosphere the droplet is said to be evapourating. When more molecules enter than escape, the water in the atmosphere is said to be condensing on the glass. When the rate at which these two events are equal, the droplet is said to be in equilibrium — or more precisely dynamic equilibrium to distinguish it from the static equilibrium of a stationary bridge or level flying airplane.

All of this blah blah is a necessary set up for the remainder of the discussion, so be patient.

What is boiling and how is it different from evapouration? Both processes involve the same liquid to gas phase transition, but where evapouration can occur at any temperature boiling occurs only at a specific temperature. Let's return to the description of evapouration just discussed.

Evapouration occurs whenever more molecules leave a liquid than enter. Condensation occurs whenever more enter than leave. These changes are driven by the concentration of liquid molecules in the atmosphere. When their concentration is low, it's more likely that molecules will leave the liquid phase than enter it, so evapouration rules. When their concentration is high, it's more likely that molecules will enter the liquid phase than leave it. When neither process dominates it must be because the atmosphere has just the right concentration of liquid molecules floating around within it — no more, no less than what it can handle. Under these circumstances the atmosphere is said to be saturated.

The most energetic vapour molecules present in the atmosphere are fighting their way into the liquid. The most energetic liquid molecules are fighting their way out into the atmosphere. There's room in the atmosphere, but it has a limit. When that's reached, evapouration stops. What we have here is a war — a war of momentum on the microscopic scale or pressure on the macroscopic scale.

A pressure cooker reduces cooking times by forcing water to remain a liquid at temperatures much higher than would be possible in an ordinary pot.

- A liquid can be made to boil;
- by increasing it's temperature to the boiling point under environmental pressure;
- by reducing the environmental pressure until boiling point equals the temperature of the liquid;
- The bubbles that form during boiling contain vapour of the liquid. This phenomena is called nucleation. Bubbles form at nucleation sites; typically, small imperfections in the walls of the container or grains of solid material;
- Cavitation is the formation of bubbles in a liquid by mechanical means; typically, rapid rotation or vibration of an immersed solid surface like a propeller or in the vortices behind an object immersed in a liquid with a high flow speed (v > 14m/s at 1 atm is sufficient). If submarines are to "run silent", they have to keep their

propeller speeds low. Cavitation occurs whenever the local pressure in a fluid drops below its saturated vapour pressure;

- Liquids can exist at negative pressures by keeping them under tension;
- The sublimation temperature of water ice is 198 K under Martian atmospheric conditions;
- The sublimation temperature of ice in a vacuum is 152 K (seems too small);
- water from deep sea thermal vents can be as hot as 700 °F and yet not boil;
- the boiling point of water decreases 1 °F for every 500 foot increase in altitude;
- 1856 Gail Borden received first patent on condensed milk from the United States and England.
- vapours can be condensed by compression alone, gases must also be cooled.
- anomalous behaviour of water, expands upon freezing.

Normal Sublimation Temperatures of Selected Materials material	**T_s (°C)**
acetylene	-84
carbon	3652
carbon dioxide	-78.5
dye sublimation printer film	205~210
graphite	3825
naphthalene	48
phosphorous, red	416
silicon carbide	2700
sulfur hexafluoride	-63.8
uranium hexafluoride	56

Phases and Solutes

Salt depresses the melting point of water making it an effective deicer at moderately low temperatures.

Unorganized Thoughts

- It has been known since the Sixteenth Century that salt lowers the freezing point of water, and the Eighteenth Century managed to reach -33 °C by exploiting this fact.
- anti-freeze/coolant
- Equilibrium can be used to describe two very different situations.
- Static equilibrium occurs whenever the components of forces and torques acting in one direction are balanced by the components of forces and torques acting in the opposite direction.
- A system in static equilibrium will have a constant translational and angular velocity.
- Dynamic equilibrium occurs whenever a change in the statistical behavior of a large group of particles is balanced by an opposite change in the statistical behavior of a similarly large group of different particles.
- A system in dynamic equilibrium will have a constant mass, pressure, temperature, and volume.
- Dynamic equilibrium is a state where no macroscopic change is observed.
- Phase changes occur whenever a large group of particles is out of dynamic equilibrium.
- The dynamic equilibrium phase plotted on a pressure-temperature graph is called a phase diagram.
- Each substance has its own characteristic phase diagram.
- The lines separating phases on a phase diagram are known as phase boundaries.

- liquid-gas.
- The liquid-gas phase boundary is known as the vapourization curve or vapour pressure curve.
- The value of the liquid-gas phase boundary at a given pressure is a boiling point.
- The value of the liquid-gas phase boundary at atmospheric pressure is the normal boiling point.
- The liquid-gas phase boundary terminates at a critical point with a critical pressure and critical temperature.
- A gas cannot be liquefied by compression if it is hotter than its critical temperature. It will remain a gas.
- solid-liquid.
- The solid-liquid phase boundary is known as the fusion curve or melting curve.
- The value of the solid-liquid phase boundary at a given pressure is a melting point (or freezing point).
- The value of the solid-liquid phase boundary at atmospheric pressure is the normal melting point (or normal freezing point).
- solid-gas.
- The solid-gas phase boundary is known as the sublimation curve.
- The value of the solid-gas phase boundary at a given pressure is a sublimation point.
- The value of the solid-gas phase boundary at atmospheric pressure is the normal sublimation point.
- The point where three phase boundaries meet is a triple point.
- All three phases exist in dynamic equilibrium when a substance is at its triple point.

- A gas cannot be liquefied by cooling if the pressure is less than the triple point pressure. It will go directly to the solid phase.

Gas Phase Reactions

The simplest chemical reactions are those that occur in the gas phase in a single step, such as the transfer of a chlorine atom from $ClNO_2$ to NO to form NO_2 and ClNO.

$$ClNO_2(g) + NO(g)'' \rightleftharpoons NO_2(g) + ClNO(g)$$

This reaction can be understood by writing the Lewis structures for all four components of the reaction. Both NO and NO_2 contain an odd number of electrons. Both NO and NO_2 can therefore combine with a neutral chlorine atom to form a molecule in which all of the electrons are paired. This reaction therefore involves the transfer of a chlorine atom from one molecule to another, as shown in the figure below.

The figure below combines a plot of the disappearance of the $ClNO_2$ consumed in this reaction with a plot of the appearance of NO_2 formed in the reaction.

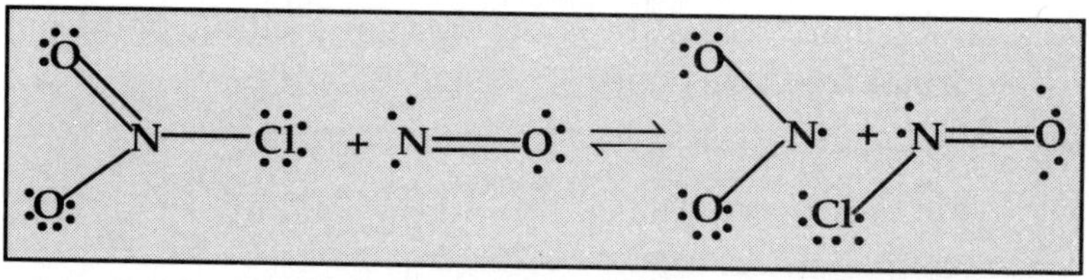

The combines a plot of the disappearance of the $ClNO_2$ consumed in this reaction with a plot of the appearance of NO_2 formed in the reaction.

One of the goals of collecting these data is to describe the rate of reaction, which is the rate at which the reactants are transformed into the products of the reaction.

The mathematical equation that describes the rate of a chemical reaction is called the rate law for the reaction. The data in the figure above are consistent with the following rate law for this reaction.

Rate = $k(ClNO_2)(NO)$

According to this rate law, the rate at which $ClNO_2$ and NO are converted into NO_2 and ClNO is proportional to the product of the concentrations of the two reactants. Initially, the rate of reaction is fast. As the reactants are converted into products, however, the $ClNO_2$ and NO concentrations become smaller, and the reaction slows down. We might expect the reaction to stop when it runs out of either $ClNO_2$ or NO. In practice, the reaction stops before this happens. This is a very fast reaction the concentration of $ClNO_2$ drops by a factor of two in less than a second. And yet, no matter how long we wait, some residual $ClNO_2$ and NO remains in the reaction flask.

A Collision Theory Model for Gas-Phase Reactions

The fact that the following reaction

$$ClNO_2(g) + NO(g) \rightleftharpoons NO_2(g) + ClNO(g)$$

seems to stop before all of the reactants are consumed can be explained with a model of chemical reactions known as the collision theory. This model assumes that $ClNO_2$ and NO molecules must collide before a chlorine atom can be transferred from one molecule to the other.

This assumption explains why the rate of the reaction is proportional to the concentration of both $ClNO_2$ and NO.

Rate = $k(ClNO_2)(NO)$

The number of collisions per second between $ClNO_2$ and NO molecules depends on their concentrations. As $ClNO_2$ and NO are consumed in the reaction, the number of collisions per second between these molecules becomes smaller, and the reaction slows down.

Suppose that we start with a mixture of $ClNO_2$ and NO, but no NO_2 or ClNO. The only reaction that can occur at first is the transfer of a chlorine atom from $ClNO_2$ to NO.

$ClNO_2(g) + NO(g) \rightarrow NO_2(g) + ClNO(g)$

Eventually, NO_2 and ClNO build up in the reaction flask, and these molecules begin to collide as well. Collisions between these molecules can result in the transfer of a chlorine atom in the opposite direction.

$ClNO_2(g) + NO(g) \leftarrow NO_2(g) + ClNO(g)$

The collision theory model of chemical reactions assumes that the rate of a simple, one-step reaction is proportional to the product of the concentrations of the ions or molecules consumed in that reaction. The rate of the forward reaction is therefore proportional to the product of the concentrations of the two "reactants."

$\text{Rate}_{\text{forward}} = k_f(ClNO_2)(NO)$

The rate of the reverse reaction, on the other hand, is proportional to the concentrations of the "products" of the reaction.

$\text{Rate}_{\text{reverse}} = k_r(NO_2)(ClNO)$

Initially, the rate of the forward reaction is much larger than the rate of the reverse reaction, because the system contains $ClNO_2$ and NO, but virtually no NO_2 and ClNO.

Initially: $\text{rate}_{\text{forward}} >> \text{rate}_{\text{reverse}}$

As $ClNO_2$ and NO are consumed, the rate of the forward reaction slows down. At the same time, NO_2 and ClNO accumulate, and the reverse reaction speeds up.

If the forward reaction gradually slows down and the reverse reaction speeds up, the system eventually has to reach a point at which the rates of the forward and reverse reactions are the same.

Eventually: $\text{rate}_{\text{forward}} = \text{rate}_{\text{reverse}}$

At this point, the reaction will seem to stop. $ClNO_2$ and NO will be consumed in the forward reaction at the rate at which they are produced in the reverse reaction. The same thing will happen to NO_2 and ClNO. When the rates of the forward and reverse reactions are the same, there is no longer any change in the concentrations of the reactants or products of the reaction. In other words, the reaction is at equilibrium.

We can now see that there are two definitions of equilibrium.

1. A system in which there is no apparent change in the concentrations of the reactants and products of a reaction.
2. A system in which the rates of the forward and reverse reactions are equal.

The first definition is based on the results of experiments that tell us that some reactions seem to stop prematurely they reach a point at which no more reactants are converted into products before the limiting reagent is consumed. The other definition is based on a theoretical model of chemical reactions that explains why reactions reach equilibrium.

We can now distinguish between reactions that go to completion and those that reach equilibrium. Reactions that aren't reversible, or that strongly favor the products, are assumed to go to completion and are represented by equations that contain a single arrow.

$$2\ Mg(s) + O_2(g) \rightarrow 2\ MgO(s)$$

Reversible reactions that reach equilibrium are indicated by a pair of arrows between the two sides of the equation.

$$ClNO_2(g) + NO(g) \rightleftharpoons NO_2(g) + ClNO(g)$$

The Evolution of Multicomponent Systems at High Pressures: I. The High-Pressure, Supercritical, Gas

The thermodynamic stability of n-octane has been investigated as a function of temperature, pressure, and degree of molecular clustering at supercritical temperatures. At low pressures, the free enthalpy is shown to be always lowest in the unassociated, gas state, and the system is, in that regime, robustly resistant to clustering. At high pressures, the free enthalpy of the unassociated, gas state exceeds that of the clustered, liquid state. At the pressure at which the values of the free enthalpies of the gas and liquid states become equal, the system becomes abruptly unstable, and will then spontaneously cluster into effective "cluster-polymers," and undergo a phase transition to a liquid state. This phenomenon is a geometric effect, and occurs even at supercritical temperatures. The gas-liquid phase transition reported here is closely related to the Alder-Wainwright gas-solid phase transition, the onset of which is applied to approximate the optimal clustering parameter. This phase transition is of the class of entropicly-driven phase transitions, characterized by an increase in spatial order accompanied by an increase in entropy, and manifests an inverted latent heat of transformation, analogous to adiabatic demagnetization.

The van der Waals critical state; and the Alder-Wainwright Gas-solid Phase Transition at Supercritical Temperatures and Pressures

Approximately one hundred, forty years ago, J.D. van der Waals enunciated the first systematic analysis of the phenomenon of gas-liquid phase transitions and the equation of state which bears his name. From his analysis, and directly from the van der Waals equation, follows the prediction of a critical state at specific values of pressure and temperature at which the density of every gas experiences large fluctuations, and for greater values of temperature the gas cannot condense, regardless of how great a pressure might be applied. Every known fluid has indeed been observed to manifest a critical gas-liquid state, as predicted by the van der Waals equation, in the thermodynamic regime of modest temperatures and pressures characteristic of the near-surface of the Earth. Almost all fluids obey also the van der Waals equation of state modestly well in that same thermodynamic regime. However, it deserves to be noted that the predictions of a critical state by the van der Waals equation obtain from its properties as an equation of third degree in the variable of density. Similarly, the apparent prohibition of a phase transition at higher values of density is also a consequence of the cubic properties of that equation. Furthermore, it must be acknowledged that the van der Waals equation is not a fundamental one, nor is it even a phenomenological equation as is, for example, the famous Boltzmann transport equation The van der Waals equation is no more than an *ad hoc* statement based upon assumptions which seemed reasonable in 1870. The developments of atomic theory and statistical mechanics, have subsequently shown that the successes of the van der Waals equation obtain by accident from its reasonable approximation to general properties of fluids in regimes of dilute densities and low pressures. Such considerations must compel strong reservations about any suppositive prohibition of a gas-liquid phase transition in thermodynamic regimes far outside the experiences which led to the enunciation of the van der Waals equation.

Approximately a century later, the first serious, universal failure of the van der Waals prohibition of phase transitions at temperatures higher than that of the critical state was demonstrated by Alder and Wainwrigh in their analysis of the hard-sphere gas whereby they established the existence of a density-dependent phase transition at high pressure and at density approximately 65% of the "close-packed" value. That transition had earlier been suggested by analysis of the Kirkwood equation which also has no solutions at densities higher than that of the Alder-Wainwright transition. The statistical mechanical problem of the hard-sphere gas was subsequently examined extensively and its analytical solution obtained in closed form independently by Wertheim and

Thiele using a general formalism developed by Percus and Yevick The analysis of the hard-sphere gas applied both by Wertheim and Thiele develops slightly different equations of state depending upon whether the problem is addressed to define explicitly the pressure or the compressibility. However, both solutions are analytic and both give accurate predictions of the Alder-Wainwright results, falling closely each on opposite sides of the observed values. Although the Percus-Yevick procedure contains certain inconsistencies, the Wertheim-Thiele solution was later derived independently and consistently in a much simpler fashion by Reiss and his coworkers who developed scaled particle theory. The formalism of scaled particle theory is based upon first principles and contains no adjustable parameters. A modified equation of state was developed later by Carnahan and Starling which uses a rational combination of the pressure and compressibility solutions from Wertheim and Thiele and the solution from scaled particle theory, and which fits the observed values of density with good accuracy throughout the domain of that variable to the transition value. The analysis reported here draws upon the extensive literature of the Alder-Wainwright transition, and uses the Carnahan-Starling equation throughout.

The high-density Alder-Wainwright transition has been interpreted as a gas-solid phase transition. That transition depends solely upon the entropic density terms which enter the partition function, and is independent of temperature. For the latter reason, the Alder-Wainwright gas-solid transition may occur in the supercritical regime. It is to be noted that neither of the Wertheim-Thiele equations ("pressure" or "compressibility") predict a gas-liquid phase transition, nor similarly does the Carnahan-Starling equation. A gas-liquid phase transition is characterized by a vapour-liquid equilibrium line along which the partial derivative of pressure with respect to volume at constant temperature must vanish. Neither the Alder-Wainwright nor the Wertheim-Thiele equation admits a real solution for that constraint of the vapour-liquid equilibrium line. The principal reason why those equations do not predict a gas-liquid phase transition is because each represents the system solely as a gas phase. Both the Wertheim-Thiele and the Carnahan-Starling equations obtain from a restricted partition function in which have been summed only those members of the ensemble which pertain to the gas state. These aspects of the Wertheim-Thiele and the Carnahan-Starling equations are discussed in connection with the supercritical, high-pressure, gas-liquid phase transition in the last section of this article.

The chemical potential and resulting Gibbs free enthalpy of the real fluid n-octane are examined as functions of temperature, pressure, and degree of molecular clustering. At low or modest pressures, the effects of the entropy are proportional to the temperature which is the dominant variable and determines the evolution of the system. At high pressures, the entropy depends upon the density of the system in a powerfully nonlinear fashion; and in thermodynamic regimes of pressures greater than approximately 10,000 atm, pressure becomes the dominant variable, and temperature relatively unimportant. Such results are consistent with the conclusions both of van der Waals and also of Alder and Wainwright.

At low pressures, the entropy of the system is shown to be dominated by the contributions attributable to the molar abundance, or number of particles, and their random motion, which together may be called the entropy of disorder. At high pressures, the entropy is shown to be dominated by contributions attributable to the hard-core repulsive terms in the inter-molecular potential, which may be called the entropy of exclusion. For all temperatures and molar abundances the entropy of exclusion is always negative, and that of disorder always positive. Therefore, there exists a critical bifurcation pressure below which the system evolves always toward dispersion and above which always toward concentration.

These properties will be shown in a following article to be universal for all fluids and the causal agents of a high-pressure, supercritical, first-order, gas-liquid phase transition. Such are responsible also for the phenomena of high-pressure polymerization and agglomeration.

The quantal partition function, pressure, and chemical potential of a real gas: The formalism of the Simplified Perturbed Hard Chain Theory [SPHCT]

In order to calculate the chemical potentials, and the entropy of a real gas or liquid in arbitrary regimes of temperature and pressure it is necessary to have an explicit, general expression for the partition function of the system. The formalism of the Simplified Perturbed Hard Chain Theory [SPHCT] generates from first-principles, statistical mechanical argument an analytic expression for the canonical partition function, the derivation of which is independent of any specific regime of temperature or density. Thereby the expressions for the pressure and chemical potential of a fluid developed by the SPHCT are similarly valid in any regime of temperature or density, and hold for dense liquids equally as for dilute gases Because the confidence with which any calculation is held depends upon an understanding of the basis for the validity of the formalism from which such was developed, that formalism is here briefly reviewed.

KNOBS

This keyword data block is used to redefine parameters that affect convergence of the numerical method during speciation, batch-reaction, and transport calculations. It also provides the capability to produce long, uninterpretable output files.

Explanation

Line 0: KNOBS

KNOBS is the keyword for the data block. Optionally, DEBUG.

Example Data Block

Line 0:	KNOBS	
Line 1:	-iterations	150
Line 2:	-convergence_tolerance	1e-8
Line 3:	-tolerance	1e-14
Line 4:	-step_size	10
Line 5:	-pe_step_size	5
Line 6:	-diagonal_scale	TRUE
Line 7:	-debug_diffuse_layer	TRUE
Line 8:	-debug_inverse	TRUE
Line 9:	-debug_model	TRUE
Line 10:	-debug_prep	TRUE
Line 11:	-debug_set	TRUE
Line 12:	-logfile	TRUE

Line 1: -iterations iterations

Iterations—Allows changing the maximum number of iterations. Optionally, iterations, or -i[terations].

Iterations —Positive integer limiting the maximum number of iterations used to solve the set of algebraic equations for a single calculation. Values greater than 200 are not usually effective. Default is 100.

Line 2: -convergence_tolerance convergence_tolerance

Convergence_tolerance—Changes the convergence criterion used to determine when the algebraic equations have been solved. For an element mole-balance equation, convergence is satisfied when mole balance is within convergence_tolerance times the total moles of the element (*convergence_tolerance.* T_m). When the -high_precision identifier of selected_Output is used, the convergence criterion is set to the smaller of convergence_tolerance and 1e-12. Default is 1e-8. Optionally, convergence_tolerance, or -c[onvergence_tolerance].

Line 3: -tolerance tolerance

-Tolerance—Allows changing the tolerance used by the optimization solver (subroutine Cl1) to determine numbers equal to zero. This is not the convergence criterion used to determine when the algebraic equations have been solved. Optionally, tolerance, or -t[olerance].

Tolerance —Positive, decimal number used by the optimization solver (subroutine cl1). All numbers smaller than this number are treated as zero. This number should approach the value of the least significant decimal digit that can be interpreted by the computer. The value of tolerance should be on the order of 1e-12 to 1e-15 for most computers and most simulations. Default is 1e-15 (or possibly smaller if the program is compiled with long double precision).

Line 4: -step_size step_size

-Step_size—Allows changing the maximum step size. Optionally, step_size, or -s[tep_size].

Step_size —Positive, decimal number limiting the maximum, multiplicative change in the activity of an aqueous master species on each iteration. Default is 100, that is, activities of master species may change by up to 2 orders of magnitude in a single iteration.

Line 5: -pe_step_size pe_step_size

-pe_step_size—Allows changing the maximum step size for the activity of the electron. Optionally, pe_step_size, or -p[e_step_size].

pe_step_size —Positive, decimal number limiting the maximum, multiplicative change in the conventional activity of electrons on each iteration. Normally, pe_step_size should be smaller than the step_size , because redox species are particularly sensitive to changes in pe. Default is 10, that is, $a_e^{-?}$ may change by up to 1 order of magnitude in a single iteration or pe may change by up to 1 unit.

Line 6: -diagonal_scale

-diagonal_scale—Allows changing the default method for scaling equations. Optionally, diagonal_scale, or -d[iagonal_scale].

—A value of true (optionally, t[rue]) indicates the alternative scaling method is to be used; false (optionally, f[alse]) indicates the alternative scaling method will not be used. If neither true nor false are entered, true is assumed. At the beginning of the run, the value is set to false. Invoking this alternative method of scaling causes any mole-balance equations with the diagonal element (approximately the total concentration of the element or element valence state in solution) less than 1e-11 to be scaled by the factor 1e-11/ (diagonal element).

Line 7: -debug_diffuse_layer

-debug_diffuse_layer—Includes debugging prints for diffuse layer calculations. This identifier applies only when -diffuse_layer is used in the SURFACE data block. Optionally, debug_diffuse_layer or -debug_d[iffuse_layer].

—A value of true (optionally, t[rue]) indicates the debugging information will be included in the output file; false (optionally, indicates debugging information will not be printed. If neither true nor false is entered, a value of true is assumed. At the start of the program, the default value is false. If this option is set to true, values of the g function—the surface excess—are printed for each value of charge for aqueous species, the charge(s) for which the value of g has not converged are printed, and the number of iterations needed for the integration, by which g values are calculated, are printed.

Line 8: -debug_inverse [(True or False)]

-debug_inverse—Includes debugging prints for subroutines called by subroutine inverse_models . Optionally, debug_inverse or -debug_i[nverse].

—A value of true (optionally, indicates the debugging information will be included in the output file; false (optionally, f[alse]) indicates debugging information will not be printed. If neither true nor false is entered, a value of true is assumed. At the start of the program, the default value is false. If this option is set to true, a large amount of information about the process of finding inverse models is printed. The program will print the following for each set of equations and inequalities that are attempted to be solved by the optimizing solver: a list of the unknowns, a list of the equations, the array that is to be solved, any nonnegativity or nonpositivity constraints on the unknowns, the solution vector, and the residual vector for the linear equations and inequality constraints. The printout is very long and very tedious.

Line 9: -debug_model

-debug_model—Includes debugging prints for subroutines called by subroutine model . Optionally, debug_model or -debug_m[odel].

—A value of true (optionally, indicates the debugging information will be included in the output file; false (optionally, f[alse]) indicates debugging information will not be printed. If neither true nor false is entered, a value of true is assumed. At the start of the program, the default value is false. If this option is set to true, a large amount of information about the Newton-Raphson equations is printed. The program will print some or all of the following at each iteration: the array that is solved, the solution vector calculated by the solver, the residuals of the linear equations and inequality constraints, the values of all of the master unknowns and their change, the moles of each pure phase and phase mole transfers, the moles of each element in the system minus the amount in pure phases and the change in this quantity. The printout is very long and very tedious. If the numerical method does not converge in iterations -1 iterations (default is after 99 iterations), this printout is automatically begun and sent to the log file phreeqc.log .

Line 10: -debug_prep

-debug_prep—Includes debugging prints for subroutine prep . Optionally, debug_prep or -debug_p[rep].

(True or False)—A value of true (optionally, t[rue]) indicates the debugging information will be included in the output file; false (optionally, f[alse]) indicates debugging information will not be printed. If neither true nor false is entered, a value of true is assumed. At the start of the program, the default value is false. If this option is set to true, the chemical equation and log K for each species and phase, as rewritten for the current calculation, are written to the output file. The printout is long and tedious.

Line 11: -debug_set

-debug_set—Includes debugging prints for subroutines called by subroutine set . Optionally, debug_set or -debug_s[et].

(True or False)—A value of true (optionally, t[rue]) indicates the debugging information will be included in the output file; false (optionally, f[alse]) indicates debugging information will not be printed. If neither true nor false is entered, a value of true is assumed. At the start of the program, the default value is false. If this option is set to true, the initial revisions of the master unknowns (see equation 84), which occur in subroutine set, are printed for each element or element valence state that fails the initial convergence criteria. The initial revisions occur before the Newton-Raphson method is invoked and attempt to provide good estimates of the master unknowns to the Newton-Raphson method. The printout is tedious.

Line 12: -logfile

-logfile—Prints information to a file named phreeqc.log. Optionally, logfile or -l[ogfile].

—A value of true (optionally, indicates information will be written to the log file, phreeqc.log ; false (optionally indicates information will not be written. If neither true nor false is entered, a value of true is assumed. At the start of the program, the default value is false. If this option is set to true, information about each calculation will be written to the log file. The information includes number of iterations in revising the initial estimates of the master unknowns, the number of Newton-Raphson iterations, and the iteration at which any infeasible solution was encountered while solving the system of nonlinear equations. (An infeasible solution occurs if no solution to the equality and inequality constraints can be found.) At each iteration, the identity of any species that exceeds 30 mol (an unreasonably large number) is written to the log file and noted as an "overflow".

Preface

❑❑❑